LENOIR-RHYNE COLLEGE
ἡ ἀλήθεια ἐλευθερώσει ὑμᾶς
1891
HICKORY, N.C.

By Sir A. Quiller-Couch

On the Art of Writing

Studies in Literature

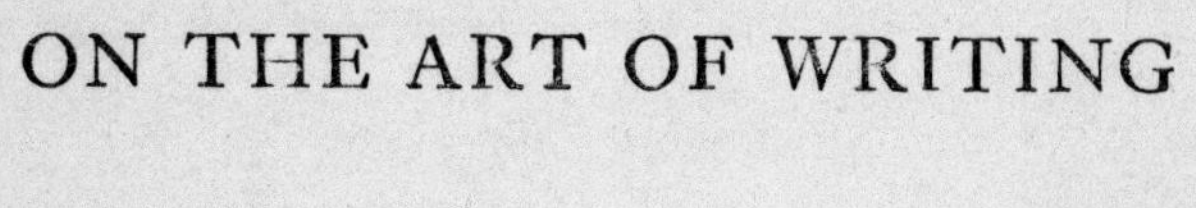

ON THE ART OF WRITING

ON THE ART OF WRITING

BY

SIR ARTHUR QUILLER-COUCH, M.A.

Fellow of Jesus College

King Edward VII Professor of English Literature

New York: G. P. Putnam's Sons
Cambridge, England: University Press

Printed in the United States of America

To

JOHN HAY LOBBAN

PREFACE

By recasting this series of lectures, which were delivered in the University of Cambridge in 1913-1914, I might with pains have turned them into a smooth treatise. But I prefer to leave them (bating a very few corrections and additions) as they were delivered. If, as the reader will all too easily detect, they abound no less in repetitions than in arguments dropped and left at loose ends—the whole bewraying a man called unexpectedly to a post where in the act of adapting himself, of learning that he might teach, he had often to adjourn his main purpose and skirmish with difficulties—they will be the truer to life; and so may experimentally enforce their preaching, that the Art of Writing is a living business.

Bearing this in mind, the reader will perhaps excuse certain small vivacities, sallies that meet fools with their folly, masking the main attack. *That*, we will see, is serious enough; and others will carry it on, though my effort come to naught.

It amounts to this—Literature is not a mere Science, to be studied; but an Art, to be practised. Great as is our own literature, we must consider it as a legacy to be improved. Any nation that potters with any glory of its past, as a thing dead and done for, is to that extent renegade. If that be granted, not all our pride in a Shakespeare can excuse the relaxation of an effort—however vain and hopeless—to better him, or some part of him. If, with all our native exemplars to give us courage, we persist in striving to write well, we can easily resign to other nations all the secondary fame to be picked up by commentators.

Recent history has strengthened, with passion and scorn, the faith in which I wrote the following pages.

ARTHUR QUILLER-COUCH.

November, 1915.

CONTENTS

PAGE

I.—Inaugural 1

II.—The Practice of Writing . . 26

III.—On the Difference between Verse and Prose 52

IV.—On the Capital Difficulty of Verse. 76

V.—Interlude: On Jargon . . . 100

VI.—On the Capital Difficulty of Prose. 127

VII.—Some Principles Reaffirmed . . 153

VIII.—On the Lineage of English Literature (I) 176

IX.—On the Lineage of English Literature (II) 201

X.—English Literature in our Universities (I) 230

XI.—English Literature in our Universities (II) 258

XII.—On Style 278

Index 299

On the Art of Writing

I

Inaugural

In all the long quarrel set between philosophy and poetry I know of nothing finer, as of nothing more pathetically hopeless, than Plato's return upon himself in his last dialogue, *The Laws*. There are who find that dialogue (left unrevised) insufferably dull, as no doubt it is without form and garrulous. But I think they will read it with a new tolerance, maybe even with a touch of feeling, if upon second thoughts they recognise in its twistings and turnings, its prolixities and repetitions, the scruples of an old man who, knowing that his time in this world is short, would not go out of it pretending to know more than he does, and even in matters concerning which he was once very sure has come to divine that, after all, as Renan says, "La Verité consiste dans les nuances."

Certainly "the mind's dark cottage battered and decayed" does in that last dialogue admit some wonderful flashes,

> For Heaven descended to the low-roofed house
> Of Socrates,

or rather to that noble "banquet-hall deserted" which aforetime had entertained Socrates.

Suffer me, Mr. Vice-Chancellor and Gentlemen, before reaching my text, to remind you of the characteristically beautiful setting. The place is Crete, and the three interlocutors—Cleinias a Cretan, Megillus a Lacedæmonian, and an Athenian stranger—have joined company on a pilgrimage to the cave and shrine of Zeus, from whom Minos, first lawgiver of the island, had reputedly derived not only his parentage but much parental instruction. Now the day being hot, even scorching, and the road from Cnossus to the Sacred Cave a long one, our three pilgrims, who have forgathered as elderly men, take it at their leisure and propose to beguile it with talk upon Minos and his laws. "Yes, and on the way," promises the Cretan, "we shall come to cypress-groves exceedingly tall and fair, and to green meadows, where we may repose ourselves and converse." "Good," assents the Athenian. "Ay, very good indeed, and better still when we arrive at them. Let us push on."

So they proceed. I have said that all three are elderly men; that is, men who have had their opportunities, earned their wages, and so nearly earned their discharge that now, looking back on life, they can afford to see Man for what he really is—at his best a noble plaything for the gods. Yet they look forward, too, a little wistfully. They are of the world, after all, and nowise so tired of it, albeit disillusioned, as to have lost interest in the game or in the young who will carry it on. So Minos and his laws soon get left behind, and the talk (as so often befalls with Plato) is of the perfect citizen and how to train him—of education, in short; and so, as ever with Plato, we are back at length upon the old question which he could never get out of his way—What to do with the poets?

It scarcely needs to be said that the Athenian has taken hold of the conversation, and that the others are as wax in his hands. "O Athenian stranger," Cleinias addresses him—"inhabitant of Attica I will not call you, for you seem to deserve rather the name of Athene herself, because you go back to first principles." Thus complimented, the stranger lets himself go. Yet somehow he would seem to have lost speculative nerve.

It was all very well in the "Republic," the ideal State, to be bold and declare for banishing poetry altogether. But elderly men have given up pursuing ideals; they have "seen too many leaders of revolt." Our Athenian is driving now at practice (as we say), at a well-governed State realisable on earth; and after all it is hard to chase out the poets, especially if you yourself happen to be something of a poet at heart. Hear, then, the terms on which after allowing that comedies may be performed, but only by slaves and hirelings, he proceeds to allow serious poetry

And if any of the serious poets, as they are termed, who write tragedy, come to us and say, "O strangers, may we go to your city and country, or may we not, and shall we bring with us our poetry? what is your will about these matters?"—how shall we answer the divine men? I think that our answer should be as follows:—

"Best of strangers," we will say to them, "we also, according to our ability, are tragic poets, and our tragedy is the best and noblest; for our whole state is an imitation of the best and noblest life. . . . You are poets and we are poets, both makers of the same strains, rivals and antagonists in the noblest of dramas, which true law alone can perfect, as our hope is. Do not then suppose that we shall all in a moment allow you to erect your stage in the Agora, and introduce the fair voices of your actors, speaking above our own, and permit you to harangue our women and children and the common people in language other than our own, and very often the opposite of our own. For a State would be mad which gave you this license, until the magistrates had determined whether your poetry might be recited and was fit for publication or not. Wherefore, O ye sons and scions of the softer Muses! first of all show your songs to the Magistrates and let them compare them with our own, and if they are the same or better, we will give you a chorus; but if not, then, my friends, we cannot."

Lame conclusion! Impotent compromise! How little applicable, at all events, to *our* Commonwealth! though, to be sure (you may say) we possess a relic of it in His Majesty's Licenser of Plays. As you know, there has been so much heated talk of late over the composition of the County Magistracy; yet I give you a countryman's word, sir, that I have heard many names proposed for the Commission of the Peace, and on many grounds, but never one on the ground that its owner had a conservative taste in verse!

Nevertheless, as Plato saw, we must deal with these poets somehow. It is possible (though not I think, likely) that in the ideal State there would be no literature, as it is certain there would be no professors of it; but since its invention men have never been able to rid themselves of it for any length of time. *Tamen usque recurrit.* They may forbid Apollo, but still he comes leading his choir, the Nine:

> Ἄκλητος μὲν ἔγωγε μένοιμί κεν· ἐς δὲ καλεύντων
> Θαρσήσας Μοίσαισι σὺν ἁμετέραισιν ἱκοίμαν.

And he may challenge us English boldly! For since Chaucer, at any rate, he and his train have never been ἄκλητοι to us—least of all here in Cambridge.

Nay, we know that he should be welcome. Cardinal Newman, proposing the idea of a university to the Roman Catholics of Dublin, lamented that the English language had not, like the Greek, "some definite words to express, simply and generally intellectual proficiency or perfection, such as 'health,' as used with reference to the animal frame, and 'virtue,' with reference to our moral nature." Well, it is a reproach to us that we do not possess the term: and perhaps again a reproach to us that our attempts at it—the word "culture" for instance—have been apt to take on some soil of controversy, some connotative damage from over-preaching on the one hand and impatience on the other. But we do earnestly desire the thing. We do prize that grace of intellect which sets So-and-so in our view as "a scholar and a gentleman." We do wish as many sons of this University as may be to carry forth that lifelong stamp from her precincts; and—this is my point—from our notion of such a man the touch of literary grace cannot be excluded. I put to you for a test Lucian's description of his friend Demonax:

> His way was like other people's; he mounted no high horse; he was just a man and a citizen. He indulged in no Socratic irony. But his discourse was full of Attic grace; those who heard it went away neither disgusted by servility, nor repelled by ill-tempered censure, but on the contrary lifted out of themselves by charity, and encouraged to more orderly, contented, hopeful lives.

I put it to you, sir, that Lucian needs not to say another word, but we know that Demonax had loved letters, and partly by aid of them had arrived at being such a man. No; by consent of all, literature is a nurse of noble natures, and right reading makes a full man in a sense even better than Bacon's; not replete, but complete rather, to the pattern for which Heaven designed him. In this conviction, in this hope, public-spirited men endow chairs in our universities, sure that literature is a good thing if only we can bring it to operate on young minds.

That he has in him some power to guide such operation a man must believe before accepting such a chair as this. And now, sir, the terrible moment is come when your ξένος must render some account—I will not say of himself, for that cannot be attempted—but of his business here. Well, first let me plead that while you have been infinitely kind to the stranger, feasting him and casting a gown over him, one thing not all your kindness has been able to do. With precedents, with traditions such as other professors enjoy, you could not furnish him. The Chair is a new one, or almost new, and for the present would seem to float in the void, like Mahomet's coffin. Wherefore, being one who (in my Lord Chief Justice Crewe's phrase) would "take hold of a twig or a twine-thread to uphold it"; being also prone (with Bacon) to believe that "the counsels to which Time hath not been called, Time will not ratify"; I do assure you that, had any legacy of guidance been discovered among the papers left by my predecessor, it would have been eagerly welcomed and as piously honoured. O, trust me, sir!—if any design for this Chair of English Literature had been left by Dr. Verrall, it is not I who would be setting up any new stage in your agora! But in his papers—most kindly searched for me by Mrs. Verrall—no such design can be found. He was, in truth, a stricken man when he came to the chair, and of what he would have built we can only be sure that, had it been this or had it been that, it would infallibly have borne the impress of one of the most beautiful minds of our generation. The gods saw otherwise; and for me, following him, I came to a trench and stretched my hands to a shade.

For me, then, if you put questions concerning the work of this chair, I must take example from the artist in Don Quixote, who being asked what he was painting answered modestly, "That is as it may turn out." The course is uncharted, and for sailing directions I have but these words of your ordinance.

> It shall be the duty of the Professor to deliver courses of lectures on English Literature from the age of Chaucer onwards, and otherwise to promote, so far as may be in his power, the study in the University of the subject of English Literature.

And I never even knew that English literature had a "subject"; or, rather, supposed it to have several! To resume:

> The Professor shall treat this subject on literary and critical rather than on philological and linguistic lines:

—a proviso which at any rate cuts off a cantle, large in itself, if not comparatively, of the new professor's ignorance. But I ask you to note the phrase "to promote, so far as may be in his power, the study"—not, you will observe, "to teach"; for this absolves me from raising at the start a question of some delicacy for me, as Green launched his *Prolegomena to Ethics* upon the remark that "an author who seeks to gain general confidence scarcely goes the right way to work when he begins with asking whether there really is such a subject as that of which he proposes to treat." In spite of—mark, pray, that I say *in spite of*—the activity of many learned professors, some doubt does lurk in the public mind, if, after all, English Literature can, in any ordinary sense, be taught, and if the attempts to teach it do not, after all, justify (as Wisdom is so often justified of her grandparents) the silent sapience of those old benefactors who abstained from endowing any such Chairs.

But that the study of English literature can be promoted in young minds by an elder one, that their zeal may be encouraged, their tastes directed, their vision cleared, quickened, enlarged—this, I take it, no man of experience will deny. Nay, since our two oldest universities have a habit of marking one another with interest—an interest, indeed, sometimes heightened by nervousness—I may point out that all this has been done of late years, and eminently done, by a Cambridge man you gave to Oxford. This, then, Mr. Vice-Chancellor—this or something like this, Gentlemen—is to be my task if I have the good fortune to win your confidence.

Let me, then, lay down two or three principles by which I propose to be guided. (1) For the first principle of all I put to you that in studying any work of genius we should begin by taking it *absolutely:* that is to say, with minds intent on discovering just what the author's mind intended; this being at once the obvious approach to its meaning (it's τὸ τί ἦν εἶναι, the "thing it was to be"), and the merest duty of politeness we owe to the great man addressing us. We should lay our minds open to what he wishes to tell, and if what he has to tell be noble and high and beautiful, we should surrender and let soak our minds in it.

Pray understand that in claiming, even insisting upon, the first place for this *absolute* study of a great work I use no disrespect towards those learned scholars whose labours will help you, Gentlemen, to enjoy it afterwards, in other ways and from other aspects; since I hold there is no surer sign of intellectual ill-breeding than to speak, even to feel, slightingly of any knowledge oneself does not happen to possess. Still less do I aim to persuade you that any one should be able to earn a Cambridge degree by the process (to borrow Macaulay's phrase) of reading our great authors "with his feet on the hob," a posture I have not even tried, to recommend it for a contemplative man's recreation. These editors not only set us the priceless example of learning for learning's sake: but even in practice they clear our texts for us, and afterwards—when we go more minutely into our author's acquaintance, wishing to learn all we can about him—by increasing our knowledge of detail they enhance our delight. Nay, with certain early writers—say Chaucer or Dunbar, as with certain highly allusive ones—Bacon, or Milton, or Sir Thomas Browne—some apparatus must be supplied from the start. But on the whole I think it a fair contention that such helps to studying an author are secondary and subsidiary; that, for example, with any author who by consent is less of his age than for all time, to study the relation he bore to his age may be important indeed, and even highly important, yet must in the nature of things be of secondary importance, not of the first.

But let us examine this principle a little more

attentively—for it is the palmary one. As I conceive it, that understanding of literature which we desire in our Euphues, our gracefully-minded youth, will include knowledge in varying degree, yet is itself something distinct from knowledge. Let us illustrate this upon poetry, which the most of us will allow to be the highest form of literary expression, if not of all artistic expression. Of all the testimony paid to poetry, none commands better witness than this—that, as Johnson said of Gray's *Elegy*, "it abounds with images which find a mirror in every mind, and with sentiments to which every heart returns an echo." When George Eliot said, "I never before met with so many of my own feelings expressed just as I should like them," she but repeated of Wordsworth (in homelier, more familiar fashion) what Johnson said of Gray; and the same testimony lies implicit in Emerson's fine remark that "Universal history, the poets, the romancers"—all good writers, in short—"do not anywhere make us feel that we intrude, that this is for our betters. Rather it is true that, in their greatest strokes, there we feel most at home." The mass of evidence, of which these are samples, may be summarized thus: As we dwell here between two mysteries, of a soul within and an ordered universe without, so among us are granted to dwell certain men of more delicate intellectual fibre than their fellows—men whose minds have, as it were, filaments to intercept, apprehend, conduct, translate home to us stray messages between these two mysteries, as modern telegraphy has learnt to search out, snatch, gather home human messages astray over waste waters of the ocean.

If, then, the ordinary man be done this service by the poet, that (as Dr. Johnson defines it) "he feels what he remembers to have felt before, but he feels it *with a great increase of sensibility*"; or even if, though the message be unfamiliar, it suggest to us, in Wordsworth's phrase, to "feel that we are greater than we know," I submit that we respond to it less by anything that usually passes for knowledge, than by an improvement of sensibility, a tuning up of the mind to the poet's pitch; so that the man we are proud to send forth from our schools will be remarkable less for something he can take out of his wallet and exhibit for knowledge, than for *being* something, and that "something" a man of unmistakable intellectual breeding, whose trained judgment we can trust to choose the better and reject the worse.

But since this refining of the critical judgment happens to be less easy of practice than the memorising of much that passes for knowledge—of what happened to Harriet or what Blake said to the soldier—and far less easy to examine on, the pedagogic mind (which I implore you not to suppose me confusing with the scholarly) for avoidance of trouble tends all the while to dodge or obfuscate what is essential, piling up accidents and irrelevancies before it until its very face is hidden. And we should be the more watchful not to confuse the pedagogic mind with the scholarly since it is from the scholar that the pedagogue pretends to derive his sanction; ransacking the great genuine commentators—be it a Skeat or a Masson or (may I add for old reverence' sake?) an Aldis Wright —fetching home bits of erudition, *non sua poma*, and announcing, "This *must* be the true Sion, for we found it in a wood."

Hence a swarm of little school books pullulates annually, all upside down and wrong from beginning to end; and hence a worse evil afflicts us, that the English schoolboy starts with a false perspective of any given masterpiece, his pedagogue urging, obtruding lesser things upon his vision until what is really important, the poem or the play itself, is seen in distorted glimpses, if not quite blocked out of view.

This same temptation—to remove a work of

art from the category for which the author designed it into another where it can be more conveniently studied—reaches even above the schoolmaster to assail some very eminent critics. I cite an example from a book of which I shall hereafter have to speak with gratitude as I shall always name it with respect—*The History of English Poetry*, by Dr. Courthope, sometime Professor of Poetry at Oxford. In his fourth volume, and in his estimate of Fletcher as a dramatist, I find this passage:

> But the crucial test of a play's quality is only applied when it is read. So long as the illusion of the stage gives credit to the action, and the words and gestures of the actor impose themselves on the imagination of the spectator, the latter will pass over a thousand imperfections, which reveal themselves to the reader, who, as he has to satisfy himself with the drama of silent images, will not be content if this or that in any way fall short of his conception of truth and nature,

—which seems equivalent to saying that the crucial test of the frieze of the Parthenon is its adaptability to an apartment in Bloomsbury. So long as the illusion of the Acropolis gave credit to Pheidias's design, and the sunlight of Attica imposed its delicate intended shadows edging the reliefs, the countrymen of Pericles might be tricked; but the visitor to the British Museum, as he has to satisfy himself with what happens indoors in the atmosphere of the West Central Postal Division of London, will not be content if Pheidias in any way fall short of *his* conception of truth and nature. Yet Fletcher (I take it) constructed his plays as plays; the illusion of the stage, the persuasiveness of the actor's voice, were conditions for which he wrought, and on which he had a right to rely; and, in short, any critic behaves uncritically who, distrusting his imagination to recreate the play as a play, elects to consider it in the category of something else.

In sum, if the great authors never oppress us with airs of condescension, but, like the great lords they are, put the meanest of us at our ease in their presence, I see no reason why we should pay to any commentator a servility not demanded by his master.

My next two principles may be more briefly stated.

(2) I propose next, then, that since our investigations will deal largely with style, that curiously personal thing; and since (as I have said) they cannot in their nature be readily brought to rule-of-thumb tests, and may therefore so easily be suspected of evading all tests, of being mere

dilettantism; I propose (I say) that my pupils and I rebuke this suspicion by constantly aiming at the concrete, at the study of such definite beauties as we can see presented in print under our eyes; always seeking the author's intention, but eschewing, for the present at any rate, all general definitions and theories, through the sieve of which the particular achievement of genius is so apt to slip. And having excluded them at first in prudence, I make little doubt we shall go on to exclude them in pride. Definitions, formulæ (some would add, creeds) have their use in any society in that they restrain the ordinary unintellectual man from making himself a public nuisance with his private opinions. But they go a very little way in helping the man who has a real sense of prose or verse. In other words, they are good discipline for some thyrsus-bearers, but the initiated have little use for them. As Thomas à Kempis "would rather feel compunction than understand the definition thereof," so the initiated man will say of the "Grand Style," for example—"Why define it for me?" When Viola says simply:

> I am all the daughters of my father's house,
> And all the brothers too,

or Macbeth demands of the Doctor

Canst thou not minister to a mind diseased,
Pluck from the memory a rooted sorrow . . . ?

or Hamlet greets Ophelia, reading her Book of Hours, with

Nymph, in thy orisons
Be all my sins remembered!

or when Milton tells of his dead friend how

Together both, ere the high lawns appear'd
Under the opening eyelids of the morn,
We drove afield,

or describes the battalions of Heaven

On they move
Indissolubly firm: nor obvious hill,
Nor strait'ning vale, nor wood, nor stream divide
Their perfect ranks,

or when Gray exalts the great commonplace

The boast of heraldry, the pomp of power,
And all that beauty, all that wealth e'er gave,
Await alike th' inevitable hour;
The paths of glory lead but to the grave,

or when Keats casually drops us such a line as

The journey homeward to habitual self,

or, to come down to our own times and to a living poet, when I open on a page of William Watson and read

> O ancient streams, O far descended woods,
> Full of the fluttering of melodious souls! . . .

"why then (will say the initiated one), why worry me with any definition of the Grand Style in English, when here, and here, and again here—in all these lines, simple or intense or exquisite or solemn—I recognise and feel the *thing?*"

Indeed, sir, the long and the short of the argument lie just here. Literature is not an abstract science, to which exact definitions can be applied. It is an art rather, the success of which depends on personal persuasiveness, on the author's skill to give as on ours to receive.

(3) For our third principle I will ask you to go back with me to Plato's wayfarers, whom we have left so long under the cypresses; and loth as we must be to lay hands on our father Parmenides, I feel we must treat the gifted Athenian stranger to a little manhandling. For did you not observe—though Greek was a living language and to his metropolitan mind the only language—how envious he showed himself to seal up the well, or allow it to trickle only under permit of a public analyst: to treat all innovation as suspect, even as, a hundred odd years ago, the Lyrical Ballads were suspect?

But the very hope of this chair, sir (as I conceive it), relies on the courage of the young. As literature is an art and therefore not to be pondered only, but practised, so ours is a living language and therefore to be kept alive, supple, active in all honourable use. The orator can yet sway men, the poet ravish them, the dramatist fill their lungs with salutary laughter or purge their emotions by pity or terror. The historian "superinduces upon events the charm of order." The novelist—well, even the novelist has his uses; and I would warn you against despising any form of art which is alive and pliant in the hands of men. For my part, I believe, bearing in mind Mr. Barrie's *Peter Pan* and the old bottles he renovated to hold that joyous wine, that even musical comedy, in the hands of a master, might become a thing of beauty. Of the novel, at any rate—whether we like it or not—we have to admit that it does hold a commanding position in the literature of our times, and to consider how far Mr. Lascelles Abercrombie was right the other day when he claimed, on the first page of his brilliant study of Thomas Hardy, that "the right to such a position is not to be disputed; for here, as elsewhere, the right to a position is no more than the power to maintain it." You may agree with that or you may not; you may or may not deplore the forms that literature is choosing nowadays; but there is no gainsaying that it is still very much alive. And I would say to you, Gentlemen, "Believe, and be glad that literature and the English tongue are both alive." Carlyle, in his explosive way, once demanded of his countrymen, "Shakespeare or India? If you had to surrender one to retain the other, which would you choose?" Well, our Indian Empire is yet in the making, while the works of Shakespeare are complete and purchasable in whole calf; so the alternatives are scarcely *in pari materia;* and moreover let us not be in a hurry to meet trouble half way. But in English literature, which, like India, is still in the making, you have at once an empire and an emprise. In that alone you have inherited something greater than Sparta. Let us strive, each in his little way, to adorn it.

But here at the close of my hour, the double argument, that literature is an art and English a living tongue, has led me right up to a fourth principle, the plunge into which (though I foresaw it from the first) all the coward in me rejoices at having to defer to another lecture. I conclude then, Gentlemen, by answering two suspicions, which very likely have been shaping themselves in your minds. In the first place, you will say, "It is all very well for this man to talk about 'cultivating an increased sensibility,' and the like; but we know what *that* leads to—to quackery, to æsthetic chatter: 'Isn't this pretty? Don't you admire that?'" Well, I am not greatly frightened. To begin with, when we come to particular criticism I shall endeavour to exchange it with you in plain terms; a manner which (to quote Mr. Robert Bridges's *Essay on Keats*) "I prefer, because by obliging the lecturer to say definitely what he means, it makes his mistakes easy to point out, and in this way the true business of criticism is advanced." But I have a second safeguard, more to be trusted: that here in Cambridge, with all her traditions of austere scholarship, any one who indulges in loose discinct talk will be quickly recalled to his tether. Though at the time Athene be not kind enough to descend from heaven and pluck him backward by the hair, yet the very *genius loci* will walk home with him from the lecture room, whispering monitions, cruel to be kind.

"But," you will say alternatively, "if we avoid loose talk on these matters we are embarking on a mighty difficult business." Why, to be sure we are; and that, I hope, will be half the enjoyment.

After all, we have a number of critics among whose methods we may search for help—from the Persian monarch who, having to adjudicate upon two poems, caused the one to be read to him, and at once, without ado, awarded the prize to the other, up to the great Frenchman whom I shall finally invoke to sustain my hope of building something; that is if you, Gentlemen, will be content to accept me less as a professor than as an elder brother.

The Frenchman is Sainte-Beuve, and I pay a debt, perhaps appropriately here, by quoting him as translated by the friend of mine, now dead, who first invited me to Cambridge and taught me to admire her—one Arthur John Butler, sometime a Fellow of Trinity, and later a great pioneer among Englishmen in the study of Dante. Thus while you listen to the appeal of Sainte-Beuve, I can hear beneath it a more intimate voice, not for the first time, encouraging me.

Sainte-Beuve then—*si magna licet componere parvis*—is delivering an Inaugural Lecture in the École Normale, the date being April 12, 1858. "Gentlemen," he begins, "I have written a good deal in the last thirty years; that is, I have scattered myself a good deal; so that I need to gather myself together, in order that my words may come before you with all the more freedom and confidence." That is his opening; and he ends:

As time goes on, you will make me believe that I can for my part be of some good to you; and with the generosity of your age you will repay me, in that feeling alone, far more than I shall be able to give you in intellectual freedom, in literary thought. If in one sense I bestow on you some of my experience, you will requite me, and in a more profitable manner, by the sight of your ardour for what is noble: you will accustom me to turn oftener and more willingly towards the future in your company. You will teach me again to hope.

II

The Practice of Writing

We found, Gentlemen, towards the close of our first lecture, that the argument had drawn us, as by a double chain, up to the edge of a bold leap, over which I deferred asking you to take the plunge with me. Yet the plunge must be taken, and to-day I see nothing for it but to harden our hearts.

Well, then, I propose to you that, English literature being (as we agreed) an art, with a living and therefore improvable language for its medium or vehicle, a part—and no small part—of our business is *to practise it.* Yes, I seriously propose to you that here in Cambridge we *practise writing;* that we practise it not only for our own improvement, but to make, or at least try to make, appropriate, perspicuous, accurate, persuasive writing a recognisable hall-mark of anything turned out by our English School. By all means let us study the great writers of the past for their own sakes;

but let us study them for our guidance; that we, in our turn, having (it is to be hoped) something to say in our span of time, say it worthily, not dwindling out the large utterance of Shakespeare or of Burke. Portraits of other great ones look down on you in your college halls; but while you are young and sit at the brief feast, what avails their serene gaze if it do not lift up your hearts and movingly persuade you to match your manhood to its inheritance?

I protest, Gentlemen, that if our eyes had not been sealed, as with wax, by the pedagogues of whom I spoke a fortnight ago, this one habit of regarding our own literature as a *hortus siccus*, this our neglect to practise good writing as the constant auxiliary of an Englishman's liberal education, would be amazing to you seated here to-day as it will be starkly incredible to the future historian of our times. Tell me, pray; if it concerned *Painting*—an art in which Englishmen boast a record far briefer, far less distinguished—what would you think of a similar acquiescence in the past, a like haste to presume the dissolution of aptitude and to close accounts, a like precipitancy to divorce us from the past, to rob the future of hope and even the present of lively interest? Consider, for reproof of these null men, the Discourses addressed (in a pedantic age, too) by Sir Joshua Reynolds to the members and students of the Royal Academy. He has (as you might expect) enough to say of Tintoretto, of Titian, of Caracci, and of the duty of studying their work with patience, with humility. But why does he exhort his hearers to con them?—Why, because he is all the time *driving at practice.* Hear how he opens his second Discourse (his first to the students). After congratulating the prize-winners of 1769, he desires "to lead them into such a course of study as may render their future progress answerable to their past improvement"; and the great man goes on:

> I flatter myself that from the long experience I have had, and the necessary assiduity with which I have pursued these studies in which like you I have been engaged, I shall be acquitted of vanity in offering some hints to your consideration. They are indeed in a great degree founded upon my own mistakes in the same pursuit. . . .

Mark the noble modesty of that! To resume—

> In speaking to you of the Theory of the Art, I shall only consider it as it has relation to the method of your studies.

And then he proceeds to preach the Old Masters. —But how?—why?—to what end? Does he recite lists of names, dates, with formulæ concerning styles? He does nothing of the sort. Does he recommend his old masters for copying, then?—for mere imitation? Not a bit of it!—he comes down like a hammer on copying. Then for what, in fine, will he have them studied? Listen:

> The more extensive your acquaintance is with the works of those who have excelled, the more extensive will be your power of *invention.*

Yes, of *invention*, your power to make something new:

> —and what may appear still more like a paradox, *the more original will be your conceptions.*

There spake Sir Joshua Reynolds; and I call that the voice of a true Elder Brother. He, standing face to face with the young, thought of the old masters mainly as spiritual begetters of practice. And will any one in this room tell me that what Reynolds said of painting is not to-day, for us, applicable to writing?

We accept it of Greek and Latin. An old sixth form master once said to me: "You may give up Latin verse for this term, if you will; but I warn you, no one can be a real scholar who does not constantly practise verse." He was mistaken, belike. I hold, for my part, that in our public schools, we give up a quite disproportionate amount of time to "composition" (of Latin prose especially) and starve the boys' reading thereby. But at any rate we do give up a large share of the time to it. Then if we insist on this way with the tongues of Homer and Virgil, why do we avoid it with the tongue of Shakespeare, our own living tongue? I answer by quoting one of the simplest wisest sayings of Don Quixote (Gentlemen, you will easily, as time goes on, and we better our acquaintance, discover my favourite authors):

> The great Homer wrote not in Latin, for he was a Greek; and Virgil wrote not in Greek, because he was a Latin. In brief, all the ancient poets wrote in the tongue which they sucked in with their mother's milk, nor did they go forth to seek for strange ones to express the greatness of their conceptions; and, this being so, it should be a reason for the fashion to extend to all nations.

Does the difference, then, perchance lie in ourselves? Will you tell me, "Oh, painting is a special art, whereas, any one can write prose passably well"? Can he, indeed?—Can *you*, sir? Nay, believe me, you are either an archangel or a very *bourgeois* gentleman indeed if you admit to having spoken English prose all your life without knowing it.

Indeed, when we try to speak prose without having practised it the result is apt to be worse than our own vernacular. How often have I heard some worthy fellow addressing a public audience—say a Parliamentary candidate who believes himself a Liberal Home Ruler, and for the moment is addressing himself to meet some criticism of the financial proposals of a Home Rule Bill. His own vernacular would be somewhat as follows:

> Oh, rot! Give the Irish their heads and they'll run straight enough. Look at the Boers, don't you know. Not half such a decent sort as the Irish. Look at Irish horses, too. Eh? What?

But this, he is conscious, would hardly suit the occasion. He therefore amends it thus:

> Mr. Chairman—er—as regards the financial proposals of His Majesty's Government, I am of the deliberate—er—opinion that our national security—I may say, our Imperial security—our security as—er—a governing people—lies in trusting the Irish as we did in the—er—case of the Boers—H'm Mr. Gladstone, Mr. Chairman—Mr. Chairman, Mr. Gladstone——

and so on. You perceive that the style is actually worse than in the sample quoted before; it has become flabby, whereas that other was at any rate nervous. But now suppose that, having practised it, our candidate was able to speak like this:

"But what," says the financier, "is peace to us without money? Your plan gives us no revenue." No? But it does—for it secures to the subject the power of refusal, the first of all revenues. Experience is a cheat, and fact is a liar, if this power in the subject of proportioning his grant, or of not granting at all, has not been found the richest mine of revenue ever discovered by the skill or by the fortune of man. It does not indeed vote you £152,750 11*s.* 2¾ *d.*, nor any other paltry limited sum—but it gives you the strong box itself, the fund, the bank, from whence only revenues can arise among a people sensible of freedom: *Positâ luditur arcâ.* . . . Is this principle to be true in England, and false everywhere else? Is it not true in Ireland? Has it not hitherto been true in the Colonies? Why should you presume that in any country a body duly constituted for any function will neglect to perform its duty and abdicate its trust? Such a presumption would go against all Government in all nations. But in truth this dread of penury of supply, from a free assembly, has no foundation in nature. For first, observe that, besides the desire which all men have naturally of supporting the honour of their own Government, that sense of dignity, and that security of property, which ever attend freedom, have a tendency to increase the stock of a free community. Most may be taken where most is accumulated. And what is the soil or climate where experience has not uniformly proved that the voluntary flow of heaped-up plenty, bursting from the weight of its own luxuriance, has ever run with a more copious stream of revenue than could be squeezed from the dry husks of oppressed indigence by the straining of all the politic machinery in the world?

That, whether you agree or disagree with its doctrine, is great prose. That is Burke. "O Athenian stranger," said the Cretan I quoted in my first lecture,—"inhabitant of Attica I will not call you, since you deserve the name of Athene herself, because you go back to first principles!"

But, you may object, "Burke is talking like a book, and I have no wish to talk like a book." Well, as a fact, Burke is here at the culmen of a long sustained argument, and his language has soared with it, as his way was—logic and emotion lifting him together as upon two balanced majestic wings. But you are shy of such heights? Very well again, and all credit to your modesty! Yet at least (I appeal to that same modesty) when you talk or write, you would wish to *observe the occasion;* to say what you have to say without impertinence or ill-timed excess. You would not harangue a drawing-room or a sub-committee, or be facetious at a funeral, or play the skeleton at a banquet; for in all such conduct you would be mixing up things that differ. Be cheerful, then, for this desire of yours *to be appropriate* is really the root of the matter. Nor do I ask you to accept this on my sole word, but will cite you the most respectable witnesses. Take, for instance, a critic who should be old enough to impress you—Dionysius of Halicarnassus. After enumerating the qualities which lend charm and nobility to style, he closes the list with "appropriateness, which all these need":

> As there is a charming diction, so there is another that is noble; as there is a polished rhythm, so there is another that is dignified; as variety adds grace in one passage, so in another it adds fulness; *and as for appropriateness, it will prove the chief source of beauty, or else of nothing at all.*

Or listen to Cicero, how he sets appropriateness in the very heart of his teaching, as the master secret:

> Is erit eloquens qui poterit parva summisse, modica temperate, magna graviter dicere. . . . Qui ad id quodcunque decebit poterit accommodare orationem. Quod quum statuerit, tum, ut quidque erit dicendum, ita dicet, nec satura jejune, nec grandia minute, nec item contra, sed erit rebus ipsis par et æqualis oratio.

—"Whatever his theme he will speak as becomes it; neither meagrely where it is copious, nor meanly where it is ample, not in *this* way where it demands *that;* but keeping his speech level with the actual subject and adequate to it."

I might quote another great man, Quintilian, to you on the first importance of this appropriateness, or "propriety"; of speaking not only to the purpose but *becomingly*—though the two (as he rightly says) are often enough one and the same thing. But I will pass on to what has ever seemed, since I found it in one of Jowett's *Introductions* to Plato, the best definition known to me of good style in literature:

> The perfection of style is variety in unity, freedom, ease, clearness, the power of saying anything, and of striking any note in the scale of human feelings, *without impropriety.*

You see, O my modest friend! that your gamut needs not to be very wide, to begin with. The point is that within it you learn to play becomingly.

Now I started by proposing that we try together to make appropriate, perspicuous, accurate, persuasive writing a hall-mark of anything turned out by our English School here, and I would add (growing somewhat hardier) a hall-mark of all Cambridge style so far as our English School can influence it. I chose these four epithets *accurate, perspicuous, persuasive, appropriate*, with some care of course, as my duty was; and will assume that by this time we are agreed to desire *appropriateness*. Now for the other three:

Perspicuity.—I shall waste no words on the need of this: since the first aim of speech is to be understood. The more clearly you write the more easily and surely you will be understood. I propose to demonstrate to you further, in a minute or so, that the more clearly you write the more clearly you will understand yourself. But a sufficient reason has been given in ten words why you should desire perspicuity.

Accuracy.—Did I not remind myself in my first lecture, that Cambridge is the home of accurate scholarship? Surely no Cambridge man would willingly be a sloven in speech, oral or written? Surely here, if anywhere, should be acknowledged of all what Newman says of the classics that "a certain unaffected neatness and propriety and grace of diction may be required of any author, for the same reason that a certain attention to dress is expected of every gentleman." After all, what are the chief differentiae between man and the brute creation but that he clothes himself, that he cooks his food, that he uses articulate speech? Let us cherish and improve all these distinctions.

But shall we now look more carefully into these twin questions of perspicuity and accuracy: for I think, pursuing them, we may almost reach the philosophic kernel of good writing. I quoted Newman playfully a moment ago. I am going to quote him in strong earnest. And here let me say that of all the books written in these hundred years there is perhaps none you can more profitably thumb and ponder than that volume of his in which, under the title of *The Idea of a University*, he collected nine discourses addressed to the Roman Catholics of Dublin with some lectures delivered to the Catholic University there. It is fragmentary, because its themes were occasional. It has missed to be appraised at its true worth, partly no doubt by reason of the colour it derives from a religion still unpopular in England. But in fact it may be read without offence by the strictest Protestant; and the book is so wise—so eminently wise—as to deserve being bound by the young student of literature for a frontlet on his brow and a talisman on his writing wrist.

Now you will find much pretty swordsmanship in its pages, but nothing more trenchant than the passage in which Newman assails and puts to rout the Persian host of infidels—I regret to say, for the most part men of science—who would persuade us that good writing, that style, is something extrinsic to the subject, a kind of ornamentation laid on to tickle the taste, a study for the dilettante, but beneath the notice of *their* stern and masculine minds.

Such a view, as he justly points out, belongs rather to the Oriental mind than to our civilisation; it reminds him of the way young gentlemen go to work in the East when they would engage in correspondence with the object of their affection. The enamoured one cannot write a sentence himself: *he* is the specialist in passion (for the moment); but thought and words are two things to him, and for words he must go to another specialist, the professional letter-writer. Thus there is a division of labour.

> The man of words, duly instructed, dips the pen of desire in the ink of devotedness and proceeds to spread it over the page of desolation. Then the nightingale of affection is heard to warble to the rose of loveliness, while the breeze of anxiety plays around the brow of expectation. That is what the Easterns are said to consider fine writing; and it seems pretty much the idea of the school of critics to which I have been referring.

Now hear this fine passage:

> Thought and speech are inseparable from each other. Matter and expression are parts of one; style is a thinking out into language. This is what I have been laying down, and this is literature; not *things*, but the verbal symbols of things; not on the other hand mere *words;* but thoughts expressed in language. Call to mind, gentlemen, the meaning of the Greek word which expresses this special prerogative of man over the feeble intelligence of the lower animals. It is called *Logos;* what does *Logos* mean? it stands both for *reason* and for *speech*, and it is difficult to say which it means more properly. It means both at once: why? because really they cannot be divided. . . . When we can separate light and illumination, life and motion, the convex and the concave of a curve, then will it be possible for thought to tread speech under foot and to hope to do without it—then will it be conceivable that the vigorous and fertile intellect should renounce its own double, its instrument of expression and the channel of its speculations and emotions.

"As if," he exclaims finely, "language were the hired servant, the mere mistress of reason, and not the lawful wife in her own house!"

If you need further argument (but what serves it to slay the slain?) let me remind you that you cannot use the briefest, the humblest process of thought, cannot so much as resolve to take your bath hot or cold, or decide what to order for breakfast, without forecasting it to yourself in some form of words. Words are, in fine, the only currency in which we can exchange thought even with ourselves. Does it not follow, then, that the more accurately we use words the closer definition we shall give to our thoughts? Does it not follow that by drilling ourselves to write perspicuously we train our minds to clarify their thought? Does it not follow that some practice in the deft use of words, with its correspondent defining of thought, may well be ancillary even to the study of natural science in a university?

But I have another word for our men of science. It was inevitable, perhaps, that Latin—so long the universal language—should cease in time to be that in which scientific works were written. It was impossible, perhaps, to substitute, by consent, some equally neat and austere modern language, such as French. But when it became an accepted custom for each nation to use its own language in scientific treatises, it certainly was not foreseen that men of science would soon be making discoveries at a rate which left their skill in words outstripped; that having to invent their terms as they went along, yet being careless and contemptuous of a science in which they have no training, they would bombast out our dictionaries with monstrously invented words that not only would have made Quintilian stare and gasp, but would affront the decently literate of any age.

After all, and though we must sigh and acquiesce in the building of Babel, we have some right to examine the bricks. I was waiting, the other day, in a doctor's anteroom, and picked up one of those books—it was a work on pathology—so thoughtfully left lying in such places; to persuade us, no doubt, to bear the ills we have rather than fly to others capable of being illustrated. I found myself engaged in following the antics of certain bacilli generically described as "antibodies." I do not accuse the author (who seemed to be a learned man) of having invented this abominable term; apparently it passed current among physiologists and he had accepted it for honest coin. I found it, later on, in Webster's invaluable dictionary: Etymology, "body" (yours or mine), "anti," up against it; compound, "antibody," a noxious microbe.

Now I do not doubt the creature thus named to be a poisonous little wretch. Those who know him may even agree that no word is too bad for him. But I am not thinking of *him*. I am thinking of *us;* and I say that for our own self-respect, whilst we retain any sense of intellectual pedigree, "antibody" is no word to throw even at a bacillus.

The man who eats peas with his knife can at least claim a historical throwback to the days when forks had but two prongs and the spoons had been removed with the soup. But "antibody" has no such respectable derivation. It is, in fact, a barbarism, and a mongrel at that. The man who uses it debases the currency of learning; and I suggest to you that it is one of the many functions of a great University to maintain the standard of that currency, to guard the *jus et norma loquendi*, to protect us from such hasty fellows or, rather, to suppeditate them in their haste.

Let me revert to our list of the qualities necessary to good writing, and come to the last—*Persuasiveness;* of which you may say, indeed, that it embraces the whole—not only the qualities of propriety, perspicuity, accuracy, we have been considering, but many another, such as harmony, order, sublimity, beauty of diction; all in short that—writing being an art, not a science, and therefore so personal a thing—may be summed up under the word *Charm.* Who, at any rate, does not seek after Persuasion? It is the aim of all the arts, and, I suppose, of all exposition of the sciences; nay, of all useful exchange of converse in our daily life. It is what Velasquez attempts in a picture, Euclid in a proposition, the Prime Minister at the Treasury box, the journalist in a leading article, our Vicar in his sermon. Persuasion, as Matthew Arnold once said, is the only true intellectual process. The mere cult of it occupied many of the best intellects of the ancients, such as Longinus and Quintilian, whose writings have been preserved to us just because they were prized. Nor can I imagine an earthly gift more covetable by you, Gentlemen, than that of persuading your fellows to listen to your views and attend to what you have at heart.

Suppose, sir, that you wish to become a journalist? Well, and why not? Is it a small thing to desire the power of influencing day by day to better citizenship an unguessed number of men, using the best thought and applying it in the best language at your command? . . . Or are you, perhaps, overawed by the printed book? On that, too, I might have a good deal to say; but for the moment would keep the question as practical as I can.

Well, it is sometimes said that Oxford men make better journalists than Cambridge men, and some attribute this to the discipline of their great School of *Literae Humaniores*, which obliges them to bring up a weekly essay to their tutor, who discusses it. Cambridge men retort that all Oxford men are journalists, and throw, of course, some accent of scorn on the word. But may I urge—and remember please that my credit is pledged to *you* now—may I urge that this is not a wholly convincing answer? For, to begin with, Oxford men have not changed their natures since leaving school, but are, by process upon lines not widely divergent from your own, much the same pleasant sensible fellows you remember. And, next if you truly despise journalism, why then despise it, have done with it and leave it alone. But I pray you, do not despise it if you mean to practise it, though it be but as a step to something better. For while the ways of art are hard at the best, they will break you if you go unsustained by belief in what you are trying to do.

In asking you to practise the written word, I began with such low but necessary things as propriety, perspicuity, accuracy. But *Persuasion*—the highest form of persuasion at any rate cannot be achieved without a sense of beauty. And now I shoot a second rapid—*I want you to practise verse, and to practise it assiduously.* . . . I am quite serious. Let me remind you that, if there ever was an ancient state of which we of Great Britain have great right and should have greater ambition to claim ourselves the spiritual heirs, that state was Imperial Rome. And of the Romans (whom you will allow to have been a practical people) nothing is more certain than the value they set upon acquiring verse. To them it was not only (as Dr. Johnson said of Greek) "like old lace—you can never have too much of it." They cultivated it with a straight eye to national improvement. Among them, as a scholar reminded us the other day, you find "an educational system deliberately and steadily directed towards the development of poetical talent. They were not a people of whom we can say, as we can of the Greeks, that they were *born to* art and literature. . . . The characteristic Roman triumphs are the triumphs of a material civilisation." Rome's rôle in the world was "the absorption of outlying genius." Themselves an unimaginative race with a language not too tractable to poetry, they made great poetry, and they made it of patient set purpose, of hard practice. I shall revert to this and maybe amplify reasons in another lecture. For the moment I content myself with stating the fact that no nation ever believed in poetry so deeply as the Romans.

Perpend this then, and do not too hastily deride my plea that you should practise verse-writing. I know most of the objections, though I may not remember all. *Mediocribus esse poetis*, etc.—that summarizes most of them; yet of an infliction of much bad verse from you, if I am prepared to endure it, why should any one else complain? I say that the youth of a university ought to practise verse-writing; and will try to bring this home to you by an argument convincing to me, though I have never seen it in print.

What are the great poetical names of the last hundred years or so? Coleridge, Wordsworth, Byron, Shelley, Landor, Keats, Tennyson, Browning, Arnold, Morris, Rossetti, Swinburne—we may stop there. Of these, all but Keats, Browning, Rossetti were university men; and of these three Keats, who died young, cut off in his prime, was the only one not fairly well-to-do. It may seem a brutal thing to say, and it is a sad thing to say: but, as a matter of hard fact, the theory that poetical genius bloweth where it listeth, and equally in poor and rich, holds little truth. As a matter of hard fact, nine out of those twelve were university men; which means that somehow or other they procured the means to get the best education England can give. As a matter of hard fact, of the remaining three you know that Browning was well-to-do, and I challenge you that, if he had not been well-to-do, he would no more have attained to writing *Saul* or *The Ring and the Book* than Ruskin would have attained to writing *Modern Painters* if his father had not dealt prosperously in business. Rossetti had a small private income; and, moreover, he painted. There remains but Keats; whom Atropos slew young, as she slew John Clare in a madhouse, and James Thomson by the laudanum he took to drug disappointment. These are dreadful facts, but let us face them. It is—however dishonouring to us as a nation—certain that, by some fault in our commonwealth, the poor poet has not in these days, nor has had for two hundred years, a dog's chance. Believe me—and I have spent a great part of the last ten years in watching some 320 elementary schools—we may prate of democracy, but actually a poor child in England has little more hope than had the son of an Athenian slave to be emancipated into that intellectual freedom of which great writings are born.

What do I argue from this? I argue that until we can bring more intellectual freedom into our State, more "joy in widest commonalty spread," upon you, a few favoured ones, rests an obligation to see that the springs of English poetry do not fail. I put it to you that of this glory of our birth and state *you* are the temporary stewards. I put it to the University, considered as a dispenser of intellectual light, that to treat English poetry as though it had died with Tennyson and your lecturers had but to compose the features of a corpse, is to abnegate high hope for the sake of a barren convenience. I put it to the Colleges, considered as disciplinary bodies, that the old way of letting Coleridge slip, chasing forth Shelley, is, after all, not the wisest way. Recollect that in poesy as in every other human business, the more there are who practise it the greater will be the chance of *someone's* reaching perfection. It is the impetus of the undistinguished host that flings forward a Diomed or a Hector. And when you point with pride to Milton's and those other mulberry trees in your Academe, bethink you "What poets are they shading to-day? Or are their leaves but feeding worms to spin gowns to drape Doctors of Letters?"

In the life of Benvenuto Cellini you will find this passage worth your pondering.—He is telling how, while giving the last touches to his *Perseus* in the great square of Florence, he and his workmen inhabited a shed built around the statue. He goes on:—

> The folk kept on attaching sonnets to the posts of the door. . . . I believe that, on the day when I opened it for a few hours to the public, more than

twenty were nailed up, all of them overflowing with the highest panegyrics. Afterwards, when I once more shut it off from view, everyone brought sonnets with Latin and Greek verses: for the University of Pisa was then in vacation, and all the doctors and scholars kept vying with each other who could produce the best.

I may not live to see the doctors and scholars of this University thus employing the long vacation; as perhaps we shall wait some time for another *Perseus* to excite them to it. But I do ask you to consider that the *Perseus* was not entirely cause nor the sonnets entirely effect; that the age when men are eager about great work is the age when great work gets itself done; nor need it disturb us that most of the sonnets were, likely enough, very bad ones—in Charles Lamb's phrase, very like what Petrarch might have written if Petrarch had been born a fool. It is the impetus that I ask of you: the will to try.

Lastly, Gentlemen, do not set me down as one who girds at your preoccupation, up here, with bodily games; for, indeed, I hold "gymnastic" to be necessary as "music" (using both words in the Greek sense) for the training of such youths as we desire to send forth from Cambridge. But I plead that they should be balanced, as they were in the perfect young knight with whose words I will conclude to-day:

Having this day my horse, my hand, my lance
  Guided so well that I obtained the prize,
  Both by the judgment of the English eyes
And of some sent from that sweet enemy France;
Horsemen my skill in horsemanship advance,
  Town-folk my strength, a daintier judge applies
  His praise to sleight which from good use doth rise;
Some lucky wits impute it but to chance;
Others, because of both sides I do take
  My blood from them who did excel in this,
Think Nature me a man-at-arms did make.
  How far they shot awry! the true cause is,
Stella looked on; and from her heavenly face
Sent forth the beams which made so fair my race.

"Untrue," you say? Well, there is truth of emotion as well as of fact; and who is there among you but would fain be able not only to win such a guerdon but to lay it in such wise at your lady's feet?

That then was Philip Sidney, called the peerless one of his age; and perhaps no Englishman ever lived more graciously or, having used life, made a better end. But you have seen this morning's newspaper; you have read of Captain Scott and his comrades, and in particular of the death of Captain Oates; and you know that the breed of Sidney is not extinct. Gentlemen, let us keep our language noble: for we still have heroes to commemorate![1]

[1] The date of the above lecture was Wednesday, February 12, 1913, the date on which our morning newspapers printed the first telegrams giving particulars of the fate of Captain Scott's heroic conquest of the South Pole and still more glorious, though defeated, return. The first brief message concerning Captain Oates, ran as follows:

"From the records found in the tent where the bodies were discovered it appeared that Captain Oates's feet and hands were badly frost-bitten, and, although he struggled on heroically, his comrades knew on March 16th that his end was approaching. He had borne intense suffering for weeks without complaint, and he did not give up hope to the very end.

"'He was a brave soul. He slept through the night hoping not to wake; but he awoke in the morning.

"'It was blowing a blizzard. Oates said: "I am just going outside and I may be some time." He went out into the blizzard, and we have not seen him since.

"'We knew that Oates was walking to his death, but though we tried to dissuade him, we knew it was the act of a brave man and an English gentleman.'"

III

On the Difference between Verse and Prose

You will forgive me, Gentlemen, that having in my second lecture encouraged you to the practice of verse as well as of prose, I seize the very next opportunity to warn you against confusing the two, which differ on some points essentially, and always so as to demand separate rules—or rather (since I am shy of the word "rules") a different concept of what the writer should aim at and what avoid. But you must, pray, understand that what follows will be more useful to the tiro in prose than to the tiro in verse; for while even a lecturer may help you to avoid writing prose in the manner of Milton, only the gods—and they hardly—can cure a versifier of being prosaic.

We started upon a promise to do without scientific definitions; and in drawing some distinctions to-day between verse and prose I shall use only a few rough ones; good, as I hope, so far as they go; not to be found contrary to your scientific ones, if ever, under another teacher you attain to them; yet for the moment used only as guides to practice, and pretending to be no more.

Thus I go some way—though by no means all the way—towards defining literature when I remind you that its very name (*litterae*—letters) implies the written rather than the spoken word; that, for example, however closely they approximate one to the other as we trace them back, and even though we trace them back to identical beginnings, the writer—the man of letters—does to-day differ from the orator. There was a time, as you know, when the poet and the historian had no less than the orator, and in the most literal sense, to "get a hearing." Nay, he got it with more pains: for the orator had his senate-house or his law-court provided, whereas Thespis jogged to fairs in a cart, and the Muse of History, like any street acrobat, had to collect her own crowd. Herodotus in search of a public packed his history in a portmanteau, carted it to Olympia, found a favourable "pitch," as we should say, and wooed an audience to him much as on a racecourse nowadays do those philanthropic gentlemen who ply a dubious trade with three half-crowns and a gold chain. It would cost us an effort to imagine the late Bishop Stubbs thus trying his fortune with a bag full of select charters at Queen's Club or at Kempton Park, and exerting his lungs to retrieve a crowd that showed some disposition to edge off towards the ring or the rails.

The historian's conditions have improved; and like any other sensible man he has advanced his claim with them, and revised his method. He writes nowadays with his eye on the printed book. He may or may not be a dull fellow: being a dull fellow, he may or may not be aware of it; but at least he knows that, if you lay him upside down on your knee, you can on awaking pick him up, resume your absorption, and even turn back some pages to discover just where or why your interest flagged: whereas a Hellene who deserted Herodotus, having a bet on the pentathlon, not only missed what he missed but missed it for life.

The invention of print, of course, has made all, or almost all, the difference.

I do not forget that the printed book—the written word—presupposes a speaking voice, and must ever have at its back some sense in us of the speaking voice. But in writing prose nowadays, while always recollecting that prose has its origin in speech—even as it behoves us to recollect that Homer intoned the *Iliad* to the harp and Sappho plucked her passion from the lyre—we have to take things as they are. Except Burns, Heine, Béranger (with Moore, if you will), and you will find it hard to compile in all the lyrical poetry of the last 150 years a list of half a dozen first-class or even second-class bards who wrote primarily *to be sung.* It may help you to estimate how far lyrical verse has travelled from its origins if you will but remind yourselves that a *sonnet* and a *sonata* were once the same thing, and that a *ballad* meant a song accompanied by dancing—the word *ballata* having been specialised down, on the one line to the *ballet*, in which Mademoiselle Genée or the Russian performers will dance for our delight, using no words at all; on the other to *Sir Patrick Spens* or *Clerk Saunders*, "ballads" to which no one in his senses would dream of pointing a toe.

Thus with verse the written (or printed) word has pretty thoroughly ousted the speaking voice and its auxiliaries—the pipe, the lute, the tabor, the chorus with its dance movements and swaying of the body; and in a quieter way much the same thing is happening to prose. In the drama, to be sure, we still write (or we should) for the actors, reckon upon their intonations, their gestures, lay account with the tears in the heroine's eyes and her visible beauty; though even in the drama to-day you may detect a tendency to substitute dialectic for action and paragraphs for the στιχομυθία, the sharp outcries of passion in its give-and-take. Again we still—some of us—deliver sermons from pulpits and orations in Parliament or upon public platforms. Yet I am told that the vogue of the sermon is passing; and (by journalists) that the leading article has largely superseded it. On that point I can offer you no personal evidence; but of civil oratory I am very sure that the whole pitch has been sensibly lowered since the day of Chatham, Burke, Sheridan; since the day of Brougham and Canning; nay ever since the day of Bright, Gladstone, Disraeli. Burke, as everyone knows, once brought down a Brummagem dagger and cast it on the floor of the House. Lord Chancellor Brougham in a peroration once knelt to the assembled peers, "*Here the noble lord inclined his knee to the Woolsack*" is, if I remember, the stage direction in Hansard. Gentlemen, though in the course of destiny one or another of you may be called upon to speak daggers to the Treasury Bench, I feel sure you will use none; while, as for Lord Brougham's genuflexions, we may agree that to emulate them would cost Lord Haldane an effort. These and even far less flagrant or flamboyant tricks of virtuosity have gone quite out of fashion. You could hardly revive them to-day and keep that propriety to which I exhorted you a fortnight ago. They would be out of tune; they would grate upon the nerves; they would offend against the whole style of modern oratory, which steadily tends to lower its key, to use the note of quiet business-like exposition, to adopt more and more the style of written prose.

Let me help your sense of this change, by a further illustration. Burke, as we know, was never shy of declaiming—even of declaiming in a torrent—when he stood up to speak; but almost as little was he shy of it when he sat down to write. If you turn to his *Letters on the Regicide Peace*—no raw compositions, but penned in his latter days and closing, or almost closing, upon that tenderest of farewells to his country—

> In this good old House, where everything at least is well aired, I shall be content to put up my fatigued horses and here take a bed for the long night that begins to darken upon me—

if, I say, you turn to these *Letters on the Regicide Peace* and consult the title-page, you will find them ostensibly addressed to "a Member of the present Parliament"; and the opening paragraphs assume that Burke and his correspondent are in general agreement. But skim the pages and your eyes will be arrested again and again by sentences like these:

> The calculation of profit in all such wars is false. On balancing the account of such wars, ten thousand hogsheads of sugar are purchased at ten thousand times their price—the blood of man should never be shed but to redeem the blood of man. It is well shed for our family, for our friends, for our God, for our country, for our kind. The rest is vanity; the rest is crime.

Magnificent truly! But your ear has doubtless detected the blank verse—three iambic lines:

> Are purchased at ten thousand times their price . . .
> Be shed but to redeem the blood of man . . .
> The rest is vanity; the rest is crime.

Again Burke catches your eye by rhetorical inversions:

> But too often different is rational conjecture from melancholy fact.

> Well is it known that ambition can creep as well as soar,

by repetitions:

> Never, no never, did Nature say one thing and Wisdom say another . . .

> Algiers is not near; Algiers is not powerful; Algiers is not our neighbour; Algiers is not infectious. Algiers, whatever it may be, is an old creation; and we have good data to calculate all the mischief to be apprehended from it. When I find Algiers transferred to Calais, I will tell you what I think of that point—

by quick staccato utterances, such as:

> And is this example nothing? It is everything. Example is the school of mankind, and they will learn at no other—

or

> Our dignity? That is gone. I shall say no more about it. Light lie the earth on the ashes of English pride!

I say that the eye or ear, caught by such tropes, must (if it be critical) recognise them at once as *rhetoric*, as the spoken word masquerading under guise of the written. Burke may pretend to be seated, penning a letter to a worthy man who will read it in his slippers; but actually Burke is up and pacing his library at Beaconsfield, now striding from fire-place to window with hands clasped under his coat tails, anon pausing to fling out an arm with some familiar accustomed gesture in a House of Commons that knows him no more, towards a Front Bench purpled by shades. In fine the pretence is Cicero writing to Atticus, but the style is Cicero denouncing Catiline.

As such it is not for your imitation. Burke happened to be a genius, with a swoop and range of mind, as of language to interpret it, with a gift to enchant, a power to strike and astound, which together make him, to my thinking, the man in our literature most nearly comparable with Shakespeare. Others may be more to your taste; you may love others better; but no other two leave you so hopeless of discovering *how it is done.* Yet not for this reason only would I warn you against imitating either. For like all great artists they accepted their conditions and wrought for them, and those conditions have changed. When Jacques wished to recite to an Elizabethan audience that

> All the world's a stage,
> And all the men and women merely players—

or Hamlet to soliloquise

> To be or not to be: that is the question—

the one did not stretch himself under a property oak, nor did the other cast himself back in a chair and dangle his legs. They both advanced boldly from the stage, down a narrow platform provided for such recitations and for that purpose built boldly forward into the auditorium, struck an attitude, declaimed the purple passage, and returned, covered with applause, to continue the action of the play. This was the theatrical convention; this the audience expected and understood; for this Shakespeare wrote. Similarly, though the device must have been wearing thin even in 1795–6, Burke cast a familiar epistle into language proper to be addressed to Mr. Speaker of the House of Commons. Shakespeare wrote, as Burke wrote, for his audience; and their glory is that they have outlasted the conditions they observed. Yet it was by observing them that they gained the world's ear. Let us, who are less than they, beware of scorning to belong to our own time.

For my part I have a great hankering to see English literature feeling back through these old modes to its origins. I think, for example, that if we studied to write verse that could really be sung, or if we were more studious to write prose that could be read aloud with pleasure to the ear, we should be opening the pores to the ancient sap; since the roots are always the roots, and we can only reinvigorate our growth through them.

Unhappily, however, I cannot preach this just yet; for we are aiming at practice, and at Cambridge (they tell me) while you speak very well, you write less expertly. A contributor to *The Cambridge Review*, a fortnight ago, lamented this at length; so you will not set the aspersion down to me, nor blame me if these early lectures too officiously offer a kind of "First Aid"; that, while all the time eager to descant on the *affinities* of speech and writing, I dwell first on their *differences;* or that, in speaking of Burke, an author I adore only "on this side idolatry," I first present him in some aspects for your avoidance. Similarly I adore the prose of Sir Thomas Browne, yet should no more commend it to you for instant imitation than I could encourage you to walk with a feather in your cap and a sword under your gown. Let us observe proprieties.

To return to Burke.—At his most flagrant, in these *Letters on the Regicide Peace*, he boldly raids Shakespeare. You are all, I doubt not, conversant with the Prologue to *Henry the Fifth:*

O for a Muse of fire, that would ascend
The brightest heaven of invention!
A kingdom for a stage, princes to act
And monarchs to behold the swelling scene!

Then should the warlike Harry, like himself,
Assume the port of Mars; and at his heels,
Leash'd in like hounds, should Famine, Sword, and Fire
Crouch for employment.

Well, this passage Burke, assuming his correspondent to be familiar with it, boldly claps into prose and inserts into a long diatribe against Pitt for having tamely submitted to the rebuffs of the French Directory. Thus it becomes:

> On that day it was thought he would have assumed the port of Mars; that he would bid to be brought forth from their hideous Kennel (where his scrupulous tenderness had too long immured them) those impatient dogs of War, whose fierce regards affright even the minister of vengeance that feeds them; that he would let them loose in Famine, Plagues, and Death, upon a guilty race to whose frame and to all whose habit, Order, Peace, Religion, and Virtue, are alien and abhorrent.

Now Shakespeare is but apologising for the shortcomings of his playhouse, whereas Burke is denouncing his country's shame and prophesying disaster to Europe. Yet do you not feel with me that while Shakespeare, using great words on the lowlier subject, contrives to make them appropriate, with Burke, writing on the loftier subject, the same or similar words have become tumid, turgid?

Why? I am sure that the difference lies not in the two men; nor is it all the secret, or even half the secret, that Burke is mixing up the spoken with the written word, using the one while pretending to use the other. That has carried us some way; but now let us take an important step farther. The root of the matter lies in certain essential differences between verse and prose. We will keep, if you please, to our rough practical definitions. Literature—the written word—is a permanent record of memorable speech; a record, at any rate, intended to be permanent. We set a thing down in ink—we print it in a book—because we feel it to be memorable, to be worth preserving. But to set this memorable speech down we must choose one of two forms, verse or prose; and I define verse to be a record in metre and rhythm, prose to be a record which, dispensing with metre (abhorring it indeed), uses rhythm laxly, preferring it to be various and unconstrained, so always that it convey a certain pleasure to the ear.

You observe that I avoid the term poetry, over which the critics have waged, and still are waging, a war that promises to be endless. Is Walt Whitman a poet? Is the Song of Songs (which is not Solomon's)—is the Book of Job—are the Psalms —all of these as rendered in our Authorized Version of Holy Writ—are all of these poetry? Well "yes," if you want my opinion; and again "yes," I am sure. But truly on this field, though scores of great men have fought across it—Sidney, Shelley, Coleridge, Scaliger (I pour the names on you at random), Johnson, Wordsworth, the two Schlegels, Aristotle with Twining his translator, Corneille, Goethe, Warton, Whately, Hazlitt, Emerson, Hegel, Gummere—but our axles grow hot. Let us put on the brake; for in practice the dispute comes to very little; since literature is an art and treats scientific definitions as J. K. Stephen recommended. From them

> It finds out what it cannot do,
> And then it goes and does it.

I am journeying, say, in the west of England. I cross a bridge over a stream dividing Devon from Cornwall. These two counties, each beautiful in its way, are quite unlike in their beauty; yet nothing happened as I stepped across the brook, and for a mile or two or even ten I am aware of no change. Sooner or later that change will break upon the mind and I shall be startled, awaking suddenly to a land of altered features. But at what turn of the road this will happen, just how long the small multiplied impressions will take to break into surmise, into conviction—that nobody can tell. So it is with poetry and prose. They are different realms, but between them lies a debatable land which a De Quincey or a Whitman or a Paul Fort or a Marinetti may attempt. I advise you who are beginners to keep well one side or other of the frontier, remembering that there is plenty of room and what happened to Tupper.

If we restrict ourselves to the terms "verse" and "prose," we shall find the line much easier to draw. Verse is memorable speech set down in metre with strict rhythms; prose is memorable speech set down without constraint of metre and in rhythms both lax and various—so lax, so various, that until quite recently no real attempt has been made to reduce them to rule. I doubt, for my part, if they can ever be reduced to rule; and after a perusal of Professor Saintsbury's latest work, *A History of English Prose Rhythm*, I am left doubting. I commend this book to you as one that clears up large patches of forest. No one has yet so well explained what our prose writers, generation after generation, have tried to do with prose; and he has, by the way, furnished us with a capital anthology—or, as he puts it, with "divers delectable draughts of example." But the road still waits to be driven. Seeking practical guidance—help for our present purpose—I note first that many a passage he scans in one way may as readily be scanned in another; that when he has finished with one and can say proudly with Wordsworth:—

> I've measured it from side to side,
> 'Tis three feet long and two feet wide,

we still have a sensation of coming out (our good master with us) by that same door wherein we went; and I cannot as yet after arduous trial discover much profit in his table of feet—pæons, dochmiacs, antispasts, proceleusmatics, and the rest—an antispast being but an iamb followed by a trochee, and proceleusmatic but two pyrrhics, or four consecutive short syllables—when I reflect that, your possible number of syllables being as many as five to a foot, you may label them (as Aristotle would say) until you come to infinity, where desire fails, without getting nearer any rule of application.

Let us respect a genuine effort of learning, though we may not detect its immediate profit. In particular let us respect whatever Professor

Saintsbury writes, who has done such splendid work upon English verse-prosody. I dare say he would retort upon my impatience grandly enough, quoting Walt Whitman:—

I am the teacher of athletes;
He that by me spreads a wider breast than my own proves the width of my own;
He most honours my style who learns under it to destroy the teacher.

His speculations may lead to much in time; though for the present they yield us small instruction in the path we seek.

It is time we harked back to our own sign-posts. Verse is written in metre and strict rhythm; prose, without metre and with the freest possible rhythm. That distinction seems simple enough, but it carries consequences very far from simple. Let me give you an illustration taken almost at hazard from Milton, from the Second Book of *Paradise Regained:*—

Up to a hill anon his steps he reared
From whose high top to ken the prospect round,
If cottage were in view, sheep-cote or herd;
But cottage, herd, or sheep-cote, none he saw.

These few lines are verse, are obviously verse with the accent of poetry; while as obviously they are mere narrative and tell us of the simplest possible incident—how Christ climbed a hill to learn what could be seen from the top. Yet observe, line for line and almost word for word, how strangely they differ from prose. Mark the inversions: "Up to a hill anon his steps he reared," "But cottage, herd, or sheep-cote, none he saw." Mark next the diction—"his steps he reared." In prose we should not rear our steps up the Gogmagog hills, or even more Alpine fastnesses; nor, arrived at the top, should we "ken" the prospect round; we might "con," but should more probably "survey" it. Even "anon" is a tricky word in prose, though I deliberately palmed it off on you a few minutes ago. Mark thirdly the varied repetition, "if cottage were in view, sheep-cote or herd—but cottage, herd, or sheep-cote, none he saw." Lastly compare the whole with such an account as you or I or Cluvienus would write in plain prose:

> Thereupon he climbed a hill on the chance that the view from its summit might disclose some sign of human habitation—a herd, a sheep-cote, a cottage perhaps. But he could see nothing of the sort.

But you will ask, "*Why* should verse and prose employ diction so different? *Why* should the one invert the order of words in a fashion not permitted to the other?" and I shall endeavour to answer these questions together with a third, which, I dare say, you have sometimes been minded to put when you have been told—and truthfully told—by your manuals and histories, that when a nation of men starts making literature it invariably starts on the difficult emprise of verse, and goes on to prose as by an afterthought. Why should men start upon the more difficult form and proceed to the easier? It is not their usual way. In learning to skate, for instance, they do not cut figures before practising loose and easy propulsion.

The answer is fairly simple. Literature (once more) is a record of memorable speech; it preserves in words a record of such thoughts or of such deeds as we deem worth preserving. Now if you will imagine yourself a very primitive man, lacking paper or parchment; or a slightly less primitive, but very poor, man to whom the price of parchment and ink is prohibitive; you have two ways of going to work. You can carve your words upon trees or stones (a laborious process) or you can commit them to memory and carry them about in your head; which is cheaper and handier. For an illustration, you find it useful, anticipating the tax-collector, to know how many days there are in the current month. But further you find it a nuisance and a ruinous waste of time to run off to the tribal tree or monolith whenever the calculation comes up; so you invent a formula, and you cast that formula into *verse* for the simple reason that verse, with its tags, alliterations, beat of syllables, jingle of rhymes (however your tribe has chosen to invent it), has a knack, not possessed by prose, of sticking in your head. You do not say, "Quick thy tablets, memory! Let me see—January has 31 days, February 28 days, March 31 days, April 30 days." You invent a verse:

> Thirty days hath September,
> April, June, and November . . .

Nay, it has been whispered to me, Gentlemen, that in this University some such process of memorising in verse has been applied by bold bad irreverently-minded men even to the *Evidences* of our cherished Paley.

This, you will say, is mere verse, and not yet within measurable distance of poetry. But wait! The men who said the more memorable things, or sang them—the men who recounted deeds and genealogies of heroes, plagues, and famines, assassinations, escapes from captivity, wanderings and conquests of the clan, all the "old, unhappy, far-off things and battles long ago"—the men who sang these things for their living, for a supper, a bed in the great hall, and something in their wallet to carry them on to the next lordship—these were gleemen, scops, bards, minstrels (call them how you will), a professional class who had great need of a full repertory in a land swarming with petty chieftains, and to adapt their strains to the particular hall of entertainment. It would never do, for example, to flatter the prowess of the Billings in the house of the Hoppings their hereditary foes, or to bore the Wokings (who lived where the crematorium now is) with the complicated genealogy of the Tootings; for this would have been to miss that appropriateness which I preached to you in my second lecture as a preliminary rule of good writing. Nay, when the Billings intermarried with the Tootings—when the Billings took to cooing, so to speak—a hasty blend of excerpts would be required for the *Epithalamium*. So it was all a highly difficult business, needing adaptability, a quick wit, a goodly stock of songs, a retentive memory and every artifice to assist it. Take *Widsith*, for example, the "far-travelled man." He begins:

Widsith spake: he unlocked his word-hoard.

So he had a hoard of words, you see; and he must have needed them, for he goes on:

Forþon ic maeg singan *and* secgan spell,
Maenan fore mengo in meoduhealle,
Hu me cynegode cystum dohten.
Ic waes mid Hunum *and* mid Hreð-ȝotum,
Mid Sweom *and* mid ȝeatum, *and* mid Suð-Denum.
Mid Wenlum ic waes *and* mid Waernum *and* mid Wicingum.
Mid ȝefþum ic waes *and* mid Winedum. . . .[1]

and so on for a full dozen lines. I say that the memory of such men must have needed every artifice to help it; and the chief artifice to their hand was one which also delighted the ears of their listeners. They sang or intoned to the harp.

There you get it, Gentlemen. I have purposely, skimming a wide subject, discarded much ballast; but you may read and scan and read again, and always you must come back to this, that the first poets sang their words to the harp or to some such instrument; and just there lies the secret why poetry differs from prose. The moment you

[1] Therefore I can sing and tell a tale, recount in the Mead Hall, how men of high race gave rich gifts to me. I was with Huns and with Hreth Goths, with the Swedes, and with the Geats, and with the South Danes; I was with the Wenlas, and with the Waernas, and with the Vikings; I was with the Gefthas and with the Winedae . . .

introduce music you let in emotion with all its sway upon speech. From that moment you change everything, down to the order of the words —the *natural* order of the words; and (remember this) though the harp be superseded, the voice never forgets it. You may take up a Barrack Room Ballad of Kipling's, and it is there, though you affect to despise it for a banjo or concertina:

> Ford—ford—ford of Kabul river . . .

"Bang, whang, whang goes the drum, tootle-te-tootle the fife." From the moment men introduced music they made verse a thing essentially separate from prose, from its natural key of emotion to its natural ordering of words. Do not for one moment imagine that when Milton writes:

> But cottage, herd, or sheep-cote, none he saw,

or

> Of man's first disobedience and the fruit
> Of that forbidden tree . . .

—where you must seek down five lines before you come to the verb, and then find it in the imperative mood—do not suppose for a moment that he is here fantastically shifting words, inverting phrases out of their natural order. For, as St. Paul might say, there is a natural order of prose and there is a natural order of verse. The natural order of prose is:

> I was born in the year 1632, in the City of York, of a good family, though not of that county; my father being a foreigner of Bremen, who settled in Hull.—[*Defoe.*]

Or

> Further I avow to your Highness that with these eyes I have beheld the person of William Wooton, B.D., who has written a good sizeable volume against a friend of your Governor (from whom, alas! he must therefore look for little favour) in a most gentlemanly style, adorned with the utmost politeness and civility.—[*Swift.*]

The natural order of poetry is:

> Thus with the year
> Seasons return, but not to me returns
> Day, or the sweet approach of Ev'n or Morn,
> Or sight of vernal bloom, or Summer's Rose,
> Or flocks, or herds, or human face divine.

Or

> But cottage, herd, or sheep-cote, none he saw.

And this basal difference you must have clear in your minds before, in dealing with prose or verse, you can practise either with profit or read either with intelligent delight.

IV

On the Capital Difficulty of Verse

In our last lecture, Gentlemen, we discussed the difference between verse, or metrical writing, and prose. We traced that difference (as you will remember) to Music—to the harp, the lyre, the dance, the chorus, all those first necessary accompaniments which verse never quite forgets; and we concluded that, as Music ever introduces emotion, which is indeed her proper and only means of persuading, so the natural language of verse will be keyed higher than the natural language of prose; will be keyed higher throughout and even for its most ordinary purposes—as for example, to tell us that So-and-so sailed to Troy with so many ships.

I grant you that our steps to this conclusion were lightly and rapidly taken; yet the stepping-stones are historically firm. Verse does precede prose in literature; verse does start with musical accompaniment; musical accompaniment does introduce emotion; and emotion does introduce an order of its own into speech. I grant you that we have travelled far from the days when a prose-writer, Herodotus, labelled the books of his history by the names of the nine Muses. I grant you that if you go to the Vatican and there study the statues of the Muses (noble, but of no early date) you may note that Calliope, Muse of the Epic—unlike her sisters Euterpe, Erato, Thalia—holds for symbol no instrument of music, but a stylus and a tablet. Yet the earlier Calliope, the Calliope of Homer, was a Muse of Song.

Μῆνιν ἄειδε, Θεά—

"Had I a thousand tongues, a thousand hands." —For what purpose does the poet wish for a thousand tongues, but to sing? for what purpose a thousand hands, but to pluck the wires? not to dip a thousand pens in a thousand inkpots.

I doubt, in fine, if your most learned studies will discover much amiss with the frontier we drew between verse and prose, cursorily though we ran its line. Nor am I daunted on comparing it with Coleridge's more philosophical one, which you will find in the *Biographia Literaria* (c. XVIII):

And first for the origin of metre. This I would trace to the balance in the mind effected by that spontaneous effort which strives to hold in check the workings of passion. It might be easily explained likewise in what manner this salutary antagonism is assisted by the very state which it counteracts, and how this balance of antagonism becomes organized into metre (in the usual acceptation of that term) by a supervening act of the will and judgment consciously and for the foreseen purpose of pleasure.

I will not swear to understanding precisely what Coleridge means here, though I believe that I do. But at any rate, and on the principle that of two hypotheses, each in itself adequate, we should choose the simpler, I suggest in all modesty that we shall do better with our own than with Coleridge's, which has the further disadvantage of being scarcely amenable to positive evidence. We can say with historical warrant that Sappho struck the lyre, and argue therefrom, still within close range of correction, that her singing responded to the instrument; whereas to assert that Sappho's mind "was balanced by a spontaneous effort which strove to hold in check the workings of a passion" is to say something for which positive evidence will be less handily found, whether to contradict or to support.

Yet if you choose to prefer Coleridge's explanation, no great harm will be done; since Coleridge, who may be presumed to have understood it, promptly goes on to deduce that,

> as the elements of metre owe their existence to a state of increased excitement, so the metre itself should be accompanied by the natural language of excitement,

which is precisely where we found ourselves, save that where Coleridge uses the word "excitement" we used the word "emotion."

Shall we employ an illustration before proceeding?—some sentence easily handled, some commonplace of the moralist, some copybook maxim I care not what. "Contentment breeds Happiness"—That is a proposition with which you can hardly quarrel; sententious, sedate, obviously true; provoking delirious advocacy as little as controversial heat; in short a very fair touchstone. Now hear how the lyric treats it, in these lines of Dekker:

> Art thou poor, yet hast thou golden slumbers?
> O sweet content!
> Art thou rich, yet is thy mind perplex'd?
> O punishment!
> Dost thou laugh to see how fools are vex'd
> To add to golden numbers golden numbers?
> O sweet content! O sweet, O sweet content!
> Work apace, apace, apace, apace;
> Honest labour wears a lovely face;
> Then hey, nonny nonny—hey nonny nonny!

Canst drink the water of the crystal spring?
O sweet content!
Swimst' thou in wealth, yet sink'st in thine own tears?
O punishment!
Then he that patiently want's burden bears
No burden bears, but is a king, a king!
O sweet content! O sweet, O sweet content!
Work apace, apace, apace, apace;
Honest labour wears a lovely face;
Then hey, nonny nonny—hey, nonny nonny!

There, in lines obviously written for music, you have our sedate sentence, "Contentment breeds Happiness," converted to mere emotion. Not (to use Coleridge's word) the "excitement" of it. There are but two plain indicative sentences in the two stanzas—(1) "Honest labour wears a lovely face" (used as a refrain), and (2) "Then he that patiently want's burden bears no burden bears, but is a king, a king!" (heightened emotionally by inversion and double repetition). Mark throughout how broken is the utterance; antithetical question answered by exclamations; both doubled and made more antithetical in the second stanza; with cunning reduplicated inversions to follow, and each stanza wound up by an outburst of emotional nonsense—"hey, nonny nonny—hey, nonny nonny!"—as a man might skip or whistle to himself for want of thought.

Now (still keeping to our same subject of Contentment) let us *prosify* the lyrical order of language down to the lowest pitch to which genius has been able to reduce it and still make noble verse. You have all read Wordsworth's famous Introduction to the *Lyrical Ballads*, and you know that Wordsworth's was a genius working on a theory that the languages of verse and of prose are identical. You know, too, I dare say, into what banalities that theory over and over again betrayed him: banalities such as—

> His widowed mother, for a second mate
> Espoused the teacher of the village school:
> Who on her offspring zealously bestowed
> Needful instruction,

—and the rest. Nevertheless Wordsworth was a genius; and genius working persistently on a narrow theory will now and again "bring it off" (as they say). So he, amid the flat waste of his later compositions, did undoubtedly "bring it off" in the following sonnet:—

> These times strike monied worldlings with dismay:
> Ev'n rich men, brave by nature, taint the air
> With words of apprehension and despair;
> While tens of thousands, thinking on the affray,

Men unto whom sufficient for the day
  And minds not stinted or untill'd are given,
  Sound healthy children of the God of Heaven,
Are cheerful as the rising sun in May.
What do we gather hence but firmer faith
  That every gift of noble origin
Is breath'd upon by Hope's perpetual breath;
  That Virtue and the faculties within
  Are vital; and that riches are akin
To fear, to change, to cowardice, and death?

Here, I grant, are no repetitions, no inversions. The sentences, though metrical, run straightforwardly, verb following subject, object verb, as in strict prose. In short here you have verse reduced to the order and structure of prose as nearly as a man of genius, working on a set theory, could reduce it while yet maintaining its proper emotional key. But first let me say that you will find very few like instances of success even in Wordsworth; and few indeed to set against innumerable passages wherein either his verse defies his theory and triumphs, or succumbs to it and, succumbing either drops sheer to bathos or spreads itself over dead flats of commonplace. Let me tell you next that the instances you will find in other poets are so few and so far between as to be negligible; and lastly that even such verse as the above has only to be compared with a passage of prose and its emotional pitch is at once betrayed. Take this, for example, from Jeremy Taylor:

> Since all the evil in the world consists in the disagreeing between the object and the appetite, as when a man hath what he desires not, or desires what he hath not, or desires amiss, he that compares his spirit to the present accident hath variety of instance for his virtue, but none to trouble him, because his desires enlarge not beyond his present fortune; and a wise man is placed in a variety of chances, like the nave or centre of a wheel in the midst of all the circumvolutions and changes of posture, without violence or change, save that it turns gently in compliance with its changed parts, and is indifferent which part is up, and which is down; for there is some virtue or other to be exercised whatever happens—either patience or thanksgiving, love or fear, moderation or humility, charity or contentedness.

Or, take this from Samuel Johnson:

> The fountain of contentment must spring up in the mind; and he who has so little knowledge of human nature as to seek happiness by changing anything but his own disposition, will waste his life in fruitless efforts and multiply the griefs which he purposes to remove.

Now, to be frank, I do not call that first passage very good prose. Like much of Jeremy Taylor's writing it is prose tricked out with the trappings and odds-and-ends of verse. It starts off, for example, with a brace of heroics—"Since all the evil in the world consists" . . . "between the object and the appetite." You may say, further, that the simile of the wheel, though proper enough to prose, is poetical too; that Homer might have used it ("As in a wheel the rim turns violently, while the nave, though it turns also, yet seems to be at rest"—something of that sort). Nevertheless you will agree with me that, in exchanging Wordsworth for Taylor and Johnson, we have relaxed something with the metre, something that the metre kept taut; and this something we discover to be the emotional pitch.

But let me give you another illustration, supplied (I dare say quite unconsciously) by one who combined a genuine love of verse—in which, however, he was no adept—with a sure instinct for beautiful prose. Contentment was a favourite theme with Isaak Walton; *The Compleat Angler* is packed with praise of it; and in *The Compleat Angler* occurs this well-known passage:—

But, master, first let me tell you, that very hour which you were absent from me, I sat down under a willow tree by the waterside, and considered what you had told me of the owner of that pleasant meadow in which you then left me; that he had a plentiful estate and not a heart to think so; that he had at this time many lawsuits depending, and that they both damped his mirth and took up so much of his time and thoughts that he had no leisure to take the sweet content that I, who pretended no title to them, took in his fields; for I could there sit quietly; and looking on the water, see some fishes sport themselves in the silver streams, others leaping at flies of several shapes and colours; looking on the hills, I could behold them spotted with woods and groves; looking down the meadows, could see, here a boy gathering lilies and lady-smocks, and there a girl cropping culverlocks and cowslips, all to make garlands suitable to this present month of May. These and many other field-flowers so perfumed the air that I thought that very meadow like that field in Sicily of which Diodorus speaks, where the perfumes arising from the place make all dogs that hunt in it to fall off and lose their hottest scent. I say, as I thus sat, joying in my own happy condition, and pitying this poor rich man that owned this and many other pleasant groves and meadows about me, I did thankfully remember what my Saviour said, that the meek possess the earth; or rather they enjoy what the others possess and enjoy not; for Anglers and meek quiet-spirited men are free from those high, those restless thoughts which corrode the sweets of life; and they, and they only can say as the poet has happily exprest it:

"Hail, blest estate of lowliness!
  Happy enjoyments of such minds
As, rich in self-contentedness,
  Can, like the reeds in roughest winds,
By yielding make that blow but small
At which proud oaks and cedars fall."

There you have a passage of felicitous prose culminating in a stanza of trite and fifth-rate verse. Yes, Walton's instinct is sound; for he is keying up the pitch; and verse, even when mediocre in quality, has its pitch naturally set above that of prose. So, if you will turn to your Walton and read the page following this passage, you will see that, still by a sure instinct, he proceeds from this scrap of reflective verse to a mere rollicking "catch":

Man's life is but vain, for 'tis subject to pain
  And sorrow, and short as a bubble;
'Tis a hodge-podge of business and money and care,
  And care and money and trouble . . .

—which is even worse rubbish, and yet a step upwards in emotion because Venator actually sings it to music. "Ay marry, sir, this is music indeed," approves Brother Peter; "this cheers the heart."

In this and the preceding lecture, Gentlemen, I have enforced at some length the opinion that to understand the many essential differences between verse and prose we must constantly bear in mind that verse, being metrical, keeps the character originally imposed on it by musical accompaniment and must always, however far the remove, be referred back to its origin and to the emotion which music excites.

Mr. George Bernard Shaw, having to commit his novel *Cashel Byron's Profession* to paper in a hurry, chose to cast it in blank verse as being more easily and readily written so: a performance which brilliantly illuminates a half-truth. Verse—or at any rate, unrhymed iambic verse—*is* easier to write than prose, if you care to leave out the emotion which makes verse characteristic and worth writing. I have little doubt that, had he chosen to attempt it, Mr. Shaw would have found his story still more ductile in the metre of *Hiawatha*. But the experiment proves nothing; or no more than that, all fine art costing labour, it may cost less if burlesqued in a category not its own.

Let me take an example from a work with which you are all familiar—*The Student's Handbook to the University and Colleges of Cambridge*. On p. 405 we read:—

The Medieval and Modern Languages Tripos is divided into ten sections, A, A2, B, C, D, E, F, G, H, and I. A student may take either one or two sections at the end of his second year of residence, and either one or two more sections at the end of his third or fourth year of residence; or he may take two sections at the end of his third year only. Thus this Tripos can be treated either as a divided or an undivided Tripos at the option of the candidate.

Now I do not hold that up to you for a model of prose. Still, lucidity rather than emotion being its aim, I doubt not that the composer spent pains on it; more pains than it would have cost him to convey his information metrically, thus:—

There is a Tripos that aspires to blend
The Medieval and the Modern tongues
In one red burial (Sing Heavenly Muse!)
Divided into sections A, A2,
B, C, D, E, F, G and H and I.
A student may take either one or two
(With some restrictions mention'd in a footnote)
At th' expiration of his second year:
Or of his third, or of his fourth again
Take one or two; or of his third alone
Take two together. Thus this tripos is
(Like nothing in the Athanasian Creed)
Divisible or indivisible
At the option of the candidate—Gadzooks!

This method has even some advantage over the method of prose in that it is more easily memorised; but it has, as you will admit, the one fatal flaw that it imports emotion into a theme which does not properly admit of emotion, and that so it offends against our first rule of writing—that it should be appropriate.

Now if you accept the argument so far as we have led it—that verse is by nature more emotional than prose—certain consequences would seem to follow: of which the first is that while the capital difficulty of verse consists in saying ordinary things the capital difficulty of prose consists in saying extraordinary things; that while with verse, keyed for high moments, the trouble is to manage the intervals, with prose the trouble is to manage the high moments.

Let us dwell awhile on this difference, for it is important. You remember my quoting to you in my last lecture these lines of Milton's:—

> Up to a hill anon his steps he reared
> From whose high top to ken the prospect round,
> If cottage were in view, sheep-cote or herd;
> But cottage, herd, or sheep-cote, none he saw.

We agreed that these were good lines, with the accent of poetry; but we allowed it to be a highly exalted way of telling how So-and-so climbed a hill for a better view but found none. Now obviously this exaltation does not arise immediately out of the action described (which is as ordinary as it well could be), but is *derivative*. It borrows its wings, its impetus, from a previous high moment, from the emotion proper to that moment, from the speech proper to that emotion; and these sustain us across to the next height as with the glide of an aëroplane. Your own sense will tell you at once that the passage would be merely bombastic if the poet were starting to set forth how So-and-so climbed a hill for the view—just that, and nothing else; as your own sense tells you that the swoop is from one height to another. For if bathos lay ahead, if Milton had but to relate how the Duke of York, with twenty thousand men, "marched up a hill and then marched down again," he certainly would not use diction such as:

> Up to a hill anon his steps he reared.

Even as it is, I think we must all detect a certain artificiality in the passage, and confess to some relief when Satan is introduced to us, ten lines lower down, to revivify the story. For let us note that, in the nature of things, the more adorned and involved our style (and Milton's is both ornate and involved) the more difficulty we must find with these flat pedestrian intervals. Milton may "bring it off," largely through knowing how to dodge the interval and contrive that it shall at any rate be brief; but, as Bagehot noted, when we come to Tennyson and find Tennyson in *Enoch Arden* informing us of a fish-jowter, that:—

Enoch's white horse, and Enoch's ocean-spoil
In ocean-smelling osier—

(*i. e.*, in a fish-basket)

—and his face,
Rough-reddened with a thousand winter gales,
Not only to the market town were known,
But in the leafy lanes beyond the down
Far as the portal-warding lion-whelp
And peacock-yewtree of the lonely Hall,
Whose Friday fare was Enoch's ministering,

why, then we feel that the vehicle is altogether too pompous for its load, and those who make speech too pompous for its content commit, albeit in varying degrees, the error of Defoe's religious lady who, seeing a bottle of over-ripe beer explode and cork and froth fly up to the ceiling, cried out, "O, the wonders of Omnipotent Power!" The poet who commends fresh fish to us as "ocean-spoil" can cast no stone at his brother who writes of them as "the finny denizens of the deep," or even at his cousin the journalist, who exalts the oyster into a "succulent bivalve"—

The feathered tribes on pinions cleave the air;
Not so the mackerel, and, still less, the bear!

I believe this difficulty, which verse, by nature and origin emotional, encounters in dealing with ordinary unemotional narrative, to lie as a technical reason at the bottom of Horace's advice to the writer of Epic to plunge *in medias res*, thus avoiding flat preparative and catching at once a high wind which shall carry him hereafter across dull levels and intervals. I believe that it lay—though whether consciously or not he scarcely tells us—at the bottom of Matthew Arnold's mind when, selecting certain qualities for which to praise Homer, he chose, for the very first, Homer's *rapidity*. "First," he says, "Homer is eminently rapid; and," he adds justly, "to this rapidity the elaborate movement of Miltonic blank verse is alien."

Now until one studies writing as an art, trying to discover what this or that form of it accomplishes with ease and what with difficulty, and why verse can do one thing and prose another, Arnold's choice of *rapidity* to put in the forefront of Homer's merits may seem merely capricious. "Homer (we say) has other great qualities. Arnold himself indicates Homer's simplicity, directness, nobility. Surely either one of these should be mentioned before rapidity, in itself not comparable as a virtue with either?"

But when we see that the difficulty of verse-narrative lies just *here;* that the epic poet who is rapid has met, and has overcome, the capital difficulty of his form, then we begin to do justice not only to Arnold as a critic but (which is of far higher moment) to Homer as a craftsman.

The genius of Homer in this matter is in fact something daemonic. He seems to shirk nothing; and the effect of this upon critics is bewildering. The acutest of them are left wondering how on earth an ordinary tale—say of how some mariners beached ship, stowed sail, walked ashore, and cooked their dinner—can be made so poetical. They are inclined to divide the credit between the poet and his fortunate age—"a time" suggests Pater "in which one could hardly have spoken at all without ideal effect, or the sailors pulled down their boat without making a picture 'in the great style' against a sky charged with marvels."

Well, the object of these lectures is not to explain genius. Just here it is rather to state a difficulty; to admit that, once in history, genius overcame it; yet warn you how rare in the tale of poetical achievement is such a success. Homer, indeed, stands first, if not unmatched, among poets in this technical triumph over the capital disability of annihilating flat passages. I omit Shakespeare and the dramatists; because they have only to give a stage direction "*Enter Cassius, looking lean*," and Cassius comes in looking leaner than nature; whereas Homer has in his narrative to walk Hector or Thersites on to the scene, describe him, walk him off. I grant the rapidity of Dante. It is amazing; and we may yield him all the credit for choosing (it was his genius that chose it) a subject which allowed of the very highest rapidity; since Hell, Purgatory, and Paradise, though they differ in other respects, have this in common, that they are populous and the inhabitants of each so compendiously shepherded together that the visitor can turn from one person to another without loss of time. But Homer does not escort us around a menagerie in which we can move expeditiously from one cage to another. He proposes at least, both in the *Iliad* and in the *Odyssey*, to unfold a story; and he *seems* to unfold it so artlessly that we linger on the most pedestrian intervals while he tells us, for example, what the heroes ate and how they cooked it. A modern writer would serve us a far better dinner. Homer brings us to his with our appetite all the keener for having waited and watched the spitting and roasting.

I would point out to you what art this genius conceals; how cunning is this apparent simplicity; and for this purpose let me take Homer at the extreme of his difficulty—when he has to describe a long sea-voyage.

Some years ago, in his last Oxford lectures, Mr. Froude lamented that no poet in this country had arisen to write a national epic of the great Elizabethan seamen, to culminate (I suppose) as his History culminated, in the defeat of the Armada; and one of our younger poets, Mr. Alfred Noyes, acting on this hint, has since given us an epic poem on *Drake* in twelve books. But Froude probably overlooked, as Mr. Noyes has not overcome, this difficulty of the flat interval which, while ever the bugbear of Epic, is magnified tenfold when our action takes place on the sea. For whereas the verse should be rapid and the high moments frequent, the business of seafaring is undeniably monotonous, as the intervals between port and port, sea-fight and sea-fight, must be long and lazy. Matters move more briskly in an occasional gale; but even a gale lasts, and must be ridden out; and the process of riding to a gale of wind:—

> For ever climbing up the climbing wave

—your ship taking one wave much as she takes another—is in its nature monotonous. Nay, you have only to read Falconer's *Shipwreck* to discover how much of dulness may lie enwrapped, to discharge itself, even in a first-class tempest. Courses, reckonings, trimmings of canvas—these occur in real life and amuse the simple mariner at the time. But to the reader, if he be a landsman, their repetition in narrative may easily become intolerable; and when we get down to the "trades," even the seaman sets his sail for a long spell of weather and goes to sleep. In short you cannot upon the wide Atlantic push action and reaction to and fro as upon the plains of windy Troy; nor could any but a superhuman genius make sustained poetry (say) out of Nelson's untiring pursuit of Villeneuve, which none the less was one of the most heroic feats in history.

This difficulty, inherent in navigation as a subject for the Epic Muse, has, I think, been very shrewdly detected and hit off in a parody of Mr. Noyes's poem by a young friend of mine, Mr. Wilfred Blair:—

Meanwhile the wind had changed, and Francis Drake
Put down the helm and drove against the seas—
Once more the wind changed, and the simple seaman,
Full fraught with weather wisdom, once again
Put down the helm and so drove on—*et cetera.*

Now Homer actually has performed this feat which we declare to be next to impossible. He actually does convey Odysseus from Troy to Ithaca, by a ten years' voyage too; he actually has narrated that voyage to us in plain straightforward words; and, what is more, he actually has made a superb epic of it. Yes, but when you come to dissect the *Odyssey*, what amazing artifice is found under that apparently straightforward tale!—eight years of the ten sliced out, to start with, and magnificently presented to Circe

> Where that Ææan isle forgets the main

—and (one may add), so forgetting, avoids the technical difficulties connected therewith.

Note the space given to Telemachus and his active search for the lost hero; note too how the mass of Odysseus' seafaring adventures is condensed into a reported speech—a traveller's tale at the court of Alcinoüs. Virgil borrowed this trick, you remember; and I dare to swear that had it fallen to Homer to attempt the impossible saga of Nelson's pursuit after Villeneuve he would have achieved it triumphantly—by means of a tale told in the first person by a survivor to Lady Hamilton. Note, again, how boldly (being free to deal with an itinerary of which his audience knew nothing but surmised that it comprehended a vast deal of the marvellous, spaced at irregular distances) Homer works in a shipwreck or a miracle wherever the action threatens to flag. Lessing, as you know, devoted several pages of the *Laokӧon* to the shield of Achilles; to Homer's craft in depicting it as it grew under Hephaestus' hammer; so that we are intrigued by the process of manufacture instead of being wearied by a description of the ready-made article; so also (if one may presume to add anything to Lessing) that we are cunningly flattered in a sense that the shield is being made for *us*. Well, that is one artifice out of many; but if you would gauge at all Homer's resource and subtlety in technique I recommend you to analyse the first twelve books of the *Odyssey* and count for yourselves the devices by which the poet—πολύτροπος as was never his hero—evades or hurries over each flat interval as he happens upon it.

> These things, Ulysses,
> The wise bards also
> Behold and sing.
> But O, what labour!
> O Prince, what pain!

You may be thinking, Gentlemen, that I take up a disproportionate amount of your time on such technical matters as these. But literature being an art (forgive the reiteration!) and therefore to be practised, I want us to be seeking all the time *how it is done:* to hunt out the principles on which the great artists wrought; to face, to rationalise, the difficulties by which they were confronted, and learn how they overcame the particular obstacle. Surely even for mere criticism, apart from practice, we shall equip ourselves better by seeking, so far as we may, how the thing is done than by standing at gaze before this or that masterpiece and murmuring, "Isn't that beautiful! How in the world now . . . !"

I am told that these lectures are criticised as tending to make you conceited; to encourage in you a belief that you can do things, when it were better that you merely admired. Well, I would not dishearten you by telling to what a shred of conceit, even of hope, a man can be reduced after twenty-odd years of the discipline. But I can, and do, affirm that the farther you penetrate in these discoveries the more sacred the ultimate mystery will become for you; that the better you understand the great authors as exemplars of practice, the more certainly you will realise what is the condescension of the gods.

Next time, then, we will attempt an enquiry into the capital difficulty of Prose.

V

Interlude: On Jargon

We parted, Gentlemen, upon a promise to discuss the capital difficulty of Prose, as we have discussed the capital difficulty of Verse. But, although we shall come to it, on second thoughts I ask leave to break the order of my argument and to interpose some words upon a kind of writing which, from a superficial likeness, commonly passes for prose in these days, and by lazy folk is commonly written for prose, yet actually is not prose at all; my excuse being the simple practical one that, by first clearing this sham prose out of the way, we shall the better deal with honest prose when we come to it. The proper difficulties of prose will remain; but we shall be agreed in understanding what it is, or at any rate what it is not, that we talk about. I remember to have heard somewhere of a religious body in the United States of America which had reason to suspect one of its churches of accepting spiritual consolation from a coloured preacher—an offence against the laws of the Synod—and despatched a Disciplinary Committee with power to act; and of the Committee's returning to report itself unable to take any action under its terms of reference, for that while a person undoubtedly coloured had undoubtedly occupied the pulpit and had audibly spoken from it in the Committee's presence, the performance could be brought within no definition of preaching known or discoverable. So it is with that infirmity of speech—that flux, that determination of words to the mouth, or to the pen,—which, though it be familiar to you in parliamentary debates, in newspapers, and as the staple language of Blue Books, Committees, Official Reports, I take leave to introduce to you as prose which is not prose and under its real name of Jargon.

You must not confuse this Jargon with what is called Journalese. The two overlap, indeed, and have a knack of assimilating each other's vices. But Jargon finds, maybe, the most of its votaries among good douce people who have never written to or for a newspaper in their life, who would never talk of "adverse climatic conditions" when they mean "bad weather"; who have never trifled with verbs such as "obsess," "recrudesce," "envisage," "adumbrate," or with phrases such as "the psychological moment," "the true inwardness," "it gives furiously to think." It dallies with Latinity—"sub silentio," "de die in diem," "cui bono?" (always in the sense, unsuspected by Cicero, of "What is the profit?")—but not for the sake of style. Your journalist at the worst is an artist in his way; he daubs paint of this kind upon the lily with a professional zeal; the more flagrant (or, to use his own word, arresting) the pigment, the happier is his soul. Like the Babu he is trying all the while to embellish our poor language, to make it more floriferous, more poetical—like the Babu for example who, reporting his mother's death, wrote, "Regret to inform you, the hand that rocked the cradle has kicked the bucket."

There is metaphor; *there* is ornament; *there* is a sense of poetry, though as yet groping in a world unrealised. No such gusto marks—no such zeal, artistic or professional, animates—the practitioners of Jargon, who are, most of them (I repeat), douce respectable persons. Caution is its father; the instinct to save everything and especially trouble; its mother, Indolence. It looks precise, but is not. It is, in these times, *safe:* a thousand men have said it before and not one to your knowledge had been prosecuted for it. And so, like respectability in Chicago, Jargon stalks unchecked in our midst. It is becoming the language of Parliament; it has become the medium through which Boards of Government, County Councils, Syndicates, Committees, Commercial Firms, express the processes as well as the conclusions of their thought and so voice the reason of their being.

Has a Minister to say "No" in the House of Commons? Some men are constitutionally incapable of saying no; but the Minister conveys it thus: "The answer to the question is in the negative." That means "no." Can you discover it to mean anything less, or anything more except that the speaker is a pompous person?—which was no part of the information demanded.

That is Jargon, and it happens to be accurate. But as a rule Jargon is by no means accurate, its method being to walk circumspectly around its target; and its faith, that having done so it has either hit the bull's-eye or at least achieved something equivalent, and safer.

Thus the clerk of a Board of Guardians will minute that—

> In the case of John Jenkins deceased the coffin provided was of the usual character.

Now this is not accurate. "In the case of John Jenkins deceased," for whom a coffin was supplied, it is wholly superfluous to tell us that he is deceased. But actually John Jenkins never had more than one case, and that was the coffin. The clerk says he had two,—a coffin in a case; but I suspect the clerk to be mistaken, and I am sure he errs in telling us that the coffin was of the usual character; for coffins have no character, usual or unusual.

For another example (I shall not tell you whence derived)—

> In the case of every candidate who is placed in the first class [So you see the lucky fellow gets a case as well as a first-class. He might be a stuffed animal: perhaps he is]— In the case of every candidate who is placed in the first class the class-list will show by some convenient mark (1) the Section or Sections for proficiency in which he is placed in the first class and (2) the Section or Sections (if any) in which he has passed with special distinction.

"The Section or Sections (if any)"—But how, if they are not any, could they be indicated by a mark however convenient?

> The Examiners will have regard to the style and method of the candidate's answers, and will give credit for excellence in *these respects*.

Have you begun to detect the two main vices of Jargon? The first is that it uses circumlocution rather than short straight speech. It says: "In the case of John Jenkins deceased, the coffin" when it means "John Jenkins's coffin"; and its yea is not yea, neither is its nay nay; but its answer is in the affirmative or in the negative, as the foolish and superfluous "case" may be. The second vice is that it habitually chooses vague woolly abstract nouns rather than concrete ones. I shall have something to say by-and-by about the concrete noun, and how you should ever be struggling for it whether in prose or in verse. For the moment I content myself with advising you, if you would write masculine English, never to forget the old tag of your Latin Grammar—

> Masculine will only be
> Things that you can touch and see.

But since these lectures are meant to be a course in First Aid to writing, I will content myself with one or two extremely rough rules; yet I shall be disappointed if you do not find them serviceable.

The first is: Whenever in your reading you come across one of these words, *case*, *instance*, *character*, *nature*, *condition*, *persuasion*, *degree*—whenever in writing your pen betrays you to one or another of them—pull yourself up and take thought. If it be "case" (I choose it as Jargon's dearest child—"in Heaven yclept Metonomy") turn to the dictionary, if you will, and seek out what meaning can be derived from *casus*, its Latin ancestor; then try how, with a little trouble, you can extricate yourself from that case. The odds are, you will feel like a butterfly who has discarded his chrysalis.

Here are some specimens to try your hand on:

(1) All those tears which inundated Lord Hugh Cecil's head were dry in the case of Mr. Harold Cox.

Poor Mr. Cox! left gasping in his aquarium!

(2) [From a cigar-merchant.] In any case, let us send you a case on approval.

(3) It is contended that Consols have fallen in consequence: but such is by no means the case.

"*Such*," by the way, is another spoilt child of Jargon, especially in Committee's Rules—"Co-opted members may be eligible as such; such members to continue to serve for such time as"—and so on.

(4) Even in the purely Celtic areas only in two or three cases do the Bishops bear Celtic names.

For "cases" read "dioceses."

Instance. In most instances the players were below their form.

But what were they playing at? Instances?

Character—Nature. There can be no doubt that the accident was caused through the dangerous nature of the spot, the hidden character of the by-road, and the utter absence of any warning or danger signal.

Mark the foggy wording of it all! And yet the man hit something and broke his neck! Contrast that explanation with the verdict of a coroner's jury in the west of England on a drowned postman: "We find that deceased met his death by an act of God, caused by sudden overflowing of the river Walkham and helped out by the scandalous neglect of the way-wardens."

The Aintree course is notoriously of a trying nature.
On account of its light character, purity, and age, Usher's whiskey is a whiskey that will agree with you.
Order. The mésalliance was of a pronounced order.
Condition. He was conveyed to his place of residence in an intoxicated condition.

"He was carried home drunk."

Quality and *Section.* Mr.——, exhibiting no less than five works, all of a superior quality, figures prominently in the oil section.

—This was written of an exhibition of pictures.

Degree. A singular degree of rarity prevails in the earlier editions of this romance.

That is Jargon. In prose it runs simply "The earlier editions of this romance are rare"—or "are very rare"—or even (if you believe what I take leave to doubt), "are singularly rare"; which should mean that they are rarer than the editions of any other work in the world.

Now what I ask you to consider about these quotations is that in each the writer was using Jargon to shirk prose, palming off periphrases upon us when with a little trouble he could have gone straight to the point. "A singular degree of rarity prevails," "the accident was caused through the dangerous nature of the spot," "but such is by no means the case." We may not be capable of much; but we can all write better than that, if we take a little trouble. In place of, "the Aintree course is of a trying nature" we can surely say "Aintree is a trying course" or "the Aintree course is a trying one"—just that and nothing more.

Next, having trained yourself to keep a look-out for these worst offenders (and you will be surprised to find how quickly you get into the way of it), proceed to push your suspicions out among the whole cloudy host of abstract terms. "How excellent a thing is sleep," sighed Sancho Panza; "it wraps a man round like a cloak"—an excellent example, by the way, of how to say a thing concretely; a Jargoneer would have said that "among the beneficent qualities of sleep its capacity for withdrawing the human consciousness from the contemplation of immediate circumstances may perhaps be accounted not the least remarkable." How vile a thing—shall we say?—is the abstract noun! It wraps a man's thoughts round like cotton wool.

Here is a pretty little nest of specimens, found in *The Times* newspaper by Messrs. H. W. and F. G. Fowler, authors of that capital little book *The King's English:*

> One of the most important reforms mentioned in the rescript is the unification of the organization of judicial institutions and the guarantee for all the tribunals of the independence necessary for securing to all classes of the community equality before the law.

I do not dwell on the cacophony; but, to convey a straightforward piece of news, might not the editor of *The Times* as well employ a man to write:

> One of the most important reforms is that of the Courts, which need a uniform system and to be

made independent. In this way only can men be assured that all are equal before the law.

I think he might.

A day or two ago the musical critic of the *Standard* wrote this:

MR. LAMOND IN BEETHOVEN

Mr. Frederick Lamond, the Scottish pianist, as an interpreter of Beethoven has few rivals. At this second recital of the composer's works at Bechstein Hall on Saturday afternoon he again displayed a complete sympathy and understanding of his material that extracted the very essence of æsthetic and musical value from each selection he undertook. The delightful intimacy of his playing and his unusual force of individual expression are invaluable assets, which, allied to his technical brilliancy, enable him to achieve an artistic triumph. The two lengthy Variations in E flat major (Op. 35) and in D major, the latter on the Turkish March from *The Ruins of Athens*, when included in the same programme, require a master hand to provide continuity of interest. *To say that Mr. Lamond successfully avoided moments that might at times, in these works, have inclined to comparative disinterestedness, would be but a moderate way of expressing the remarkable fascination with which his versatile playing endowed them*, but *at the same time* two of the sonatas given included a similar form of composition, and no matter how intellectually brilliant may be the interpretation, the extravagant use of a certain mode is bound in time to become somewhat ineffective. In the Three Sonatas, the E major (Op. 109), the A major (Op. 2), No. 2, and the C minor (Op. 111), Mr. Lamond signalized his perfect insight into the composer's varying moods.

Will you not agree with me that here is no writing, here is no prose, here is not even English, but merely a flux of words to the pen?

Here again is a string, a concatenation—say, rather, a tiara of gems of purest ray serene from the dark unfathomed caves of a Scottish newspaper:

> The Chinese viewpoint, as indicated in this letter, may not be without interest to your readers, because it evidently is suggestive of more than an academic attempt to explain an unpleasant aspect of things which, if allowed to materialize, might suddenly culminate in disaster resembling the Chang-Sha riots. It also ventures to illustrate incidents having their inception in recent premature endeavours to accelerate the development of Protestant missions in China; but we would hope for the sake of the interests involved that what my correspondent describes as "the irresponsible ruffian element" may be known by their various religious designations only within very restricted areas.

Well, the Chinese have given it up, poor fellows! and are asking the Christians—as to-day's newspapers inform us—to pray for them. Do you wonder? But that is, or was, the Chinese "viewpoint,"—and what a willow-pattern viewpoint!

Observe its delicacy. It does not venture to interest or be interesting; merely "to be not without interest." But it does "venture to illustrate incidents"—which, for a viewpoint, is brave enough; and this illustration "is suggestive of something more than an academic attempt to explain an unpleasant aspect of things which, if allowed to materialise, might suddenly culminate." *What* materialises? The unpleasant aspect? or the things? Grammar says the "things," "things which if allowed to materialise." But things are materialised already, and as a condition of their being things. It must be the aspect, then, that materialises. But, if so, it is also the aspect that culminates, and an aspect, however unpleasant, can hardly do that, or at worst cannot culminate in anything resembling the Chang-Sha riots. . . . I give it up.

Let us turn to another trick of jargon; the trick of Elegant Variation, so rampant in the sporting press that there, without needing to attend these lectures, the undergraduate detects it for laughter:—

> Hayward and C. B. Fry now faced the bowling, which apparently had no terrors for the Surrey crack. The old Oxonian, however, took some time in settling to work. . . .

Yes, you all recognise it and laugh at it. But why do you practise it in your essays? An undergraduate brings me an essay on Byron. In an essay on Byron, Byron is (or ought to be) mentioned many times. I expect, nay exact, that Byron shall be mentioned again and again. But my undergraduate has a blushing sense that to call Byron Byron twice on one page is indelicate. So Byron, after starting bravely as Byron, in the second sentence turns into "that great but unequal poet" and thenceforward I have as much trouble with Byron as ever Telemachus with Proteus to hold and pin him back to his proper self. Halfway down the page he becomes "the gloomy master of Newstead"; overleaf he is reincarnated into "the meteoric darling of society"; and so proceeds through successive avatars—"this arch-rebel," "the author of *Childe Harold*," "the apostle of scorn," "the ex-Harrovian, proud, but abnormally sensitive of his club-foot," "the martyr of Missolonghi," "the pageant-monger of a bleeding heart." Now this again is jargon. It does not, as most jargon does, come of laziness; but it comes of timidity, which is worse. In literature as in life he makes himself felt who not only calls a spade a spade but has the pluck to double spades and redouble.

For another rule—just as rough and ready, but just as useful: Train your suspicions to bristle up whenever you come upon "as regards," "with regard to," "in respect of," "in connection with," "according as to whether," and the like. They are all dodges of jargon, circumlocutions for evading this or that simple statement; and I say that it is not enough to avoid them nine times out of ten, or nine-and-ninety times out of a hundred. You should never use them. That is positive enough, I hope? Though I cannot admire his style, I admire the man who wrote to me, "Re Tennyson—your remarks anent his *In Memoriam* make me sick"; for though *re* is not a preposition of the first water, and "anent" has enjoyed its day, the finish crowned the work. But here are a few specimens far, very far, worse:—

The special difficulty in Professor Minocelsi's case [our old friend "case" again] arose *in connexion with* the view he holds *relative to* the historical value of the opening pages of Genesis.

That is jargon. In prose, even taking the miserable sentence as it stands constructed, we should write "the difficulty arose over the views he holds about the historical value," etc.

From a popular novelist:—

> I was entirely indifferent *as to* the results of the game, caring nothing at all *as to* whether *I had losses or gains*—

Cut out the first "as" in "as to," and the second "as to" altogether, and the sentence begins to be prose—"I was indifferent to the results of the game, caring nothing whether I had losses or gains."

But why, like Dogberry, have "had losses"? Why not simply "lose." Let us try again. "I was entirely indifferent to the results of the game, caring nothing at all whether I won or lost."

Still the sentence remains absurd; for the second clause but repeats the first without adding one jot. For if you care not at all whether you win or lose, you must be entirely indifferent to the results of the game. So why not say, "I was careless if I won or lost," and have done with it?

> A man of simple and charming character, he was fitly *associated with* the distinction of the Order of Merit.

I take this gem with some others from a collection made three years ago, by the *Oxford Magazine;* and I hope you admire it as one beyond price. "He was associated with the distinction of the

Order of Merit" means "he was given the Order of Merit." If the members of that Order make a society then he was associated with them; but you cannot associate a man with a distinction. The inventor of such fine writing would doubtless have answered Canning's Needy Knife-grinder with:—

> I associate thee with sixpence! I will see thee in another association first!

But let us close our *florilegium* and attempt to illustrate jargon by the converse method of taking a famous piece of English (say Hamlet's soliloquy) and remoulding a few lines of it in this fashion:—

> To be, or the contrary? Whether the former or the latter be preferable would seem to admit of some difference of opinion; the answer in the present case being of an affirmative or of a negative character according as to whether one elects on the one hand to mentally suffer the disfavour of fortune, albeit in an extreme degree, or on the other to boldly envisage adverse conditions in the prospect of eventually bringing them to a conclusion. The condition of sleep is similar to, if not indistinguishable from that of death; and with the addition of finality the former might be considered identical with the latter: so that in this

connection it might be argued with regard to sleep that, could the addition be effected, a termination would be put to the endurance of a multiplicity of inconveniences, not to mention a number of downright evils incidental to our fallen humanity, and thus a consummation achieved of a most gratifying nature.

That is jargon: and to write jargon is to be perpetually shuffling around in the fog and cotton-wool of abstract terms; to be for ever hearkening, like Ibsen's Peer Gynt, to the voice of the Boyg exhorting you to circumvent the difficulty, to beat the air because it is easier than to flesh your sword in the thing. The first virtue, the touchstone of masculine style, is its use of the active verb and the concrete noun. When you write in the active voice, "They gave him a silver teapot," you write as a man. When you write "He was made the recipient of a silver teapot," you write jargon. But at the beginning set even higher store on the concrete noun. Somebody—I think it was FitzGerald—once posited the question, "What would have become of Christianity if Jeremy Bentham had had the writing of the Parables?" Without pursuing that dreadful enquiry I ask you to note how carefully the Parables—those exquisite short stories—speak only of "things which you can touch and see"—"A sower went forth to sow," "The Kingdom of Heaven is like unto leaven, which a woman took,"—and not the Parables only, but the Sermon on the Mount and almost every verse of the Gospel. The Gospel does not, like my young essayist, fear to repeat a word, if the word be good. The Gospel says "Render unto Cæsar the things that are Cæsar's"—not "Render unto Cæsar the things that appertain to that potentate." The Gospel does not say "Consider the growth of the lilies," or even "Consider how the lilies grow." It says, "Consider the lilies, how they grow."

Or take Shakespeare. I wager you that no writer of English so constantly chooses the concrete word, in phrase after phrase forcing you to touch and see. No writer so insistently teaches the general through the particular. He does it even in *Venus and Adonis* (as Professor Wendell, of Harvard, pointed out in a brilliant little monograph on Shakespeare, published some ten years ago). Read any page of *Venus and Adonis* side by side with any page of Marlowe's *Hero and Leander* and you cannot but mark the contrast: in Shakespeare the definite, particular, visualised image, in Marlowe the beautiful generalisation, the abstract term, the thing seen at a literary remove. Take the two openings, both of which start out with the sunrise. Marlowe begins:—

> Now had the Morn espied her lover's steeds:
> Whereat she starts, puts on her purple weeds,
> And, red for anger that he stay'd so long,
> All headlong throws herself the clouds among.

Shakespeare wastes no words on Aurora and her feelings, but gets to his hero and to business without ado:—

> Even as the sun with purple-colour'd face—

(You have the sun visualised at once),

> Even as the sun with purple-colour'd face
> Had ta'en his last leave of the weeping morn,
> Rose-cheek'd Adonis hied him to the chase;
> Hunting he loved, but love he laugh'd to scorn.

When Shakespeare has to describe a horse, mark how definite he is:—

> Round-hoof'd, short-jointed, fetlocks shag and long,
> Broad breast, full eye, small head and nostril wide,
> High crest, short ears, straight legs and passing strong;
> Thin mane, thick tail, broad buttock, tender hide.

Or again, in a casual simile, how definite:—

> Upon this promise did he raise his chin,
> Like a dive-dipper peering through a wave,
> Which, being look'd on, ducks as quickly in.

Or take, if you will, Marlowe's description of Hero's first meeting Leander:—

> It lies not in our power to love or hate,
> For will in us is over-ruled by fate . . . ,

and set against it Shakespeare's description of Venus' last meeting with Adonis, as she came on him lying in his blood:—

> Or as a snail whose tender horns being hit
> Shrinks backward in his shelly cave with pain,
> And there, all smother'd up, in shade doth sit,
> Long after fearing to creep forth again;
>   So, at his bloody view—

I do not deny Marlowe's lines (if you will study the whole passage) to be lovely. You may even judge Shakespeare's to be crude by comparison. But you cannot help noting that whereas Marlowe steadily deals in abstract, nebulous terms, Shakespeare constantly uses concrete ones, which later on he learned to pack into verse, such as:—

> Sleep that knits up the ravell'd sleeve of care.

Is it unfair to instance Marlowe, who died young? Then let us take Webster for the comparison; Webster, a man of genius or of something very like it, and commonly praised by the critics for his mastery over definite, detailed, and what I may call *solidified sensation.* Let us take this admired passage from his *Duchess of Malfy*:—

Ferdinand. How doth our sister Duchess bear herself
In her imprisonment?
Basola. Nobly: I'll describe her.
She's sad as one long wed to 't, and she seems
Rather to welcome the end of misery
Than shun it: a behaviour so noble
As gives a majesty to adversity.[1]
You may discern the shape of loveliness
More perfect in her tears than in her smiles;
She will muse for hours together;[2] and her silence
Methinks expresseth more than if she spake.

Now set against this the well-known passage from *Twelfth Night* where the Duke asks and Viola answers a question about someone unknown to him and invented by her—a mere phantasm, in

[1] Note the abstract terms.
[2] Here we first come on the concrete: and beautiful it is.

short: yet note how much more definite is the language:—

Viola. My father had a daughter lov'd a man;
As it might be, perhaps, were I a woman,
I should your lordship.
Duke And what's her history?
Viola. A blank, my lord. She never told her love,
But let concealment, like a worm i' the bud,
Feed on her damask cheek; she pined in thought,
And with a green and yellow melancholy
She sat like Patience on a monument
Smiling at grief. Was not this love indeed?

Observe (apart from the dramatic skill of it) how, when Shakespeare *has* to use the abstract noun "concealment," on an instant it turns into a visible worm "feeding" on the visible rose; how, having to use a second abstract word "patience," at once he solidifies it in tangible stone.

Turning to prose, you may easily assure yourselves that men who have written learnedly on the art agree in treating our maxim—to prefer the concrete term to the abstract, the particular to the general, the definite to the vague—as a canon of rhetoric. Whately has much to say on it. The late Mr. E. J. Payne, in one of his admirable prefaces to Burke (prefaces too little known and valued, as too often happens to scholarship hidden away in a schoolbook), illustrated the maxim by setting a passage from Burke's speech *On Conciliation with America* alongside a passage of like purport from Lord Brougham's *Inquiry into the Policy of the European Powers*. Here is the deadly parallel:—

BURKE.

In large bodies the circulation of power must be less vigorous at the extremities. Nature has said it. The Turk cannot govern Ægypt and Arabia and Curdistan as he governs Thrace; nor has he the same dominion in Crimea and Algiers which he has in Brusa and Smyrna. Despotism itself is obliged to truck and huckster. The Sultan gets such obedience as he can. He governs with a loose rein, that he may govern at all; and the whole of the force and vigour of his authority in his centre is derived from a prudent relaxation in all his borders.

BROUGHAM.

In all the despotisms of the East, it has been observed that the further any part of the empire is removed from the capital, the more do its inhabitants enjoy some sort of rights and privileges: the more inefficacious is the power of the monarch; and the more feeble and easily decayed is the organisation of the government.

You perceive that Brougham has transferred Burke's thought to his own page; but will you not also perceive how pitiably, by dissolving Burke's vivid particulars into smooth generalities, he has enervated its hold on the mind?

"This particularising style," comments Mr. Payne, "is the essence of poetry; and in prose it is impossible not to be struck with the energy it produces. Brougham's passage is excellent in its way: but it pales before the flashing lights of Burke's sentences." The best instances of this energy of style, he adds, are to be found in the classical writers of the seventeenth century. "When South says, 'An Aristotle was but the rubbish of an Adam, and Athens but the rudiments of Paradise,' he communicates more effectually the notion of the difference between the intellect of fallen and of unfallen humanity than in all the philosophy of his sermons put together."

You may agree with me, or you may not, that South in this passage is expounding trash; but you will agree with Mr. Payne and me that he uttered it vividly.

Let me quote to you, as a final example of this vivid style of writing, a passage from Dr. John Donne far beyond and above anything that ever lay within South's compass:—

The ashes of an Oak in the Chimney are no epitaph of that Oak, to tell me how high or how large that was; it tells me not what flocks it sheltered while it stood, nor what men it hurt when it fell. The dust of great persons' graves is speechless, too; it says nothing, it distinguishes nothing. As soon the dust of a wretch whom thou wouldest not, as of a prince whom thou couldest not look upon will trouble thine eyes if the wind blow it thither; and when a whirlewind hath blown the dust of the Churchyard into the Church, and the man sweep out the dust of the Church into the Churchyard, who will undertake to sift those dusts again and to pronounce, This is the Patrician, this is the noble flowre [flour], this the yeomanly, this the Plebeian bran? So is the death of *Iesabel* (*Iesabel* was a Queen) expressed. They shall not say *This is Iesabel:* not only not wonder that it is, nor pity that it should be; but they shall not say, they shall not know, *This is Iesabel.*

Carlyle noted of Goethe, "his emblematic intellect, his never-failing tendency to transform into *shape*, into *life*, the feeling that may dwell in him. Everything has form, has visual excellence: the poet's imagination bodies forth the forms of things unseen, and his pen turns them into shape."

Perpend this, Gentlemen, and maybe you will not hereafter set it down to my reproach that I wasted an hour of a May morning in a denunciation of jargon, and in exhorting you upon a technical matter at first sight so trivial as the choice between abstract and definite words.

A lesson about writing your language may go deeper than language; for language (as in a former lecture I tried to preach to you) is your reason, your λόγος. So long as you prefer abstract words, which express other men's summarised concepts of things, to concrete ones which lie as near as can be reached to things themselves and are the first-hand material for your thoughts, you will remain, at the best, writers at second-hand. If your language be jargon, your intellect, if not your whole character, will almost certainly correspond. Where your mind should go straight, it will dodge: the difficulties it should approach with a fair front and grip with a firm hand it will be seeking to evade or circumvent. For the style is the man, and where a man's treasure is there his heart, and his brain, and his writing, will be also.

VI

On the Capital Difficulty of Prose

TO-DAY, Gentlemen, leaving the Vanity Fair of Jargon behind us, we have to essay a difficult country; of which, though fairly confident of his compass-bearings, your guide confesses that wide tracts lie outside his knowledge—outside of anything that can properly be called his knowledge. I feel indeed somewhat as Gideon must have felt when he divided his host on the slopes of Mount Gilead, warning back all who were afraid. In asking the remnant to follow as attentively as they can, I promise only that, if Heaven carry us safely across, we shall have "broken the back" of the desert.

In my last lecture but one, then,—and before our small interlude with jargon—the argument had carried us, more or less neatly, up to this point: that the capital difficulty of verse consisted in saying ordinary unemotional things, of bridging the flat intervals between high moments. This point, I believe, we made effectively enough.

Now, for logical neatness, we should be able to oppose a corresponding point, that the capital difficulty of prose consists in saying extraordinary things, in running it up from its proper level to these high emotional, musical, moments. And mightily convenient that would be, Gentlemen, if I were here to help you to answer scientific questions about prose and verse instead of helping you, in what small degree I can, to write. But in Literature (which, let me remind you yet once again, is an art) you cannot classify as in a science.

Pray attend while I impress on you this most necessary warning. In studying literature, and still more in studying to write it, distrust all classification! All classifying of literature intrudes "science" upon an art, and is artificially "scientific"; a trick of pedants, that they may make it the easier to examine you on things with which no man should have any earthly concern, as I am sure he will never have a heavenly one. Beetles, minerals, gases, may be classified; and to have them classified is not only convenient but a genuine advance of knowledge. But if you had to *make* a beetle, as men are making poetry, how much would classification help? To classify in a science is necessary for the purpose of that science: to classify when you come to art is at the best an expedient, useful to some critics and to a multitude of examiners. It serves the art-critic to talk about Tuscan, Flemish, Pre-Raphaelite, schools of painting. The expressions are handy, and we know more or less what they intend. Just so handily it may serve us to talk about "Renaissance poets," "the Elizabethans," "the Augustan age." But such terms at best cannot be scientific, precise, determinate, as for examples the terms "inorganic," "mammal," "univalve," "Old Red Sandstone" are scientific, precise, determinate. An animal is either a mammal or it is not: you cannot say as assuredly that a man is or is not an Elizabethan. We call Shakespeare an Elizabethan and the greatest of Elizabethans, though as a fact he wrote his most famous plays when Elizabeth was dead. Shirley was but seven years old when Elizabeth died; yet (if "Elizabethan" have any meaning but a chronological one) Shirley belongs to the Elizabethan firmament, albeit but as a pale star low on the horizon: whereas Donne—a post-Elizabethan if ever there was one—had by 1603 reached his thirtieth year and written almost every line of those wonderful lyrics which for a good sixty years gave the dominant note to Jacobean and Caroline poetry.

In treating of an art we classify for handiness, not for purposes of exact knowledge; and man (*improbus homo*) with his wicked inventions is for ever making fools of our formulae. Be consoled—and, if you are wise, thank Heaven—that genius uses our best-laid logic to explode it.

Be consoled, at any rate, on finding that after deciding the capital difficulty of prose to lie in saying extraordinary things, in running up to the high emotional moments, the prose-writers explode and blow our admirable conclusions to ruins.

You see, we gave them the chance to astonish us when we defined prose as "a record of human thought, dispensing with metre and using rhythm laxly." When you give genius leave to use something laxly, at its will, genius will pretty surely get the better of you.

Observe, now, following the story of English prose, what has happened. Its difficulty—the inherent, the native disability of prose—is to handle the high emotional moments which more properly belong to verse. Well, we strike into the line of our prose-writers, say as early as Malory. We come on this; of the Passing of Arthur:—

"My time hieth fast," said the king. Therefore said Arthur unto Sir Bedivere, "Take thou Excalibur my good sword, and go with it to yonder water side; and when thou comest there I charge thee throw my sword in that water and come again and tell me what there thou seest." "My lord," said Bedivere, "Your commandment shall be done; and lightly bring you word again." So Sir Bedivere departed, and by the way he beheld that noble sword, that the pommel and the haft was all of precious stones, and then he said to himself, "If I throw this rich sword in the water, thereof shall never come good, but harm and loss." And then Sir Bedivere hid Excalibur under a tree. And so, as soon as he might, he came again unto the king, and said he had been at the water and had thrown the sword into the water, "What saw thou there?" said the king. "Sir," he said, "I saw nothing but waves and winds."

Now I might say a dozen things of this and of the whole passage that follows, down to Arthur's last words. Specially might I speak to you of the music of its monosyllables—"'What saw you there?' said the king. . . . 'Do as well as thou mayest; for in me is no trust for to trust in. For I will into the Vale of Avilion, to heal me of my grievous wound. And if thou hear never more of me, pray for my soul.'" But, before making comment at all, I shall quote you another passage; this from Lord Berners' translation of Froissart, of the death of Robert Bruce:—

It fortuned that King Robert of Scotland was right sore aged and feeble: for he was greatly charged with the great sickness, so that there was no way for him but death. And when he felt that his end drew near, he sent for such barons and lords of his realm as he trusted best, and shewed them how there was no remedy with him, but he must needs leave this transitory life. . . . Then he called to him the gentle knight, Sir William Douglas, and said before all the lords, "Sir William, my dear friend, ye know well that I have had much ado in my days to uphold and sustain the right of this realm; and when I had most ado I made a solemn vow, the which as yet I have not accomplished, whereof I am right sorry; the which was, if I might achieve and make an end of all my wars, so that I might once have brought this realm in rest and peace, then I promised in my mind to have gone and warred on Christ's enemies, adversaries to our holy Christian faith. To this purpose mine heart hath ever intended, but our Lord would not consent thereto. . . . And sith it is so that my body can not go, nor achieve that my heart desireth, I will send the heart instead of the body, to accomplish mine avow. . . . I will, that as soon as I am trespassed out of this world, that ye take my heart out of my body, and embalm it, and take of my treasure as ye shall think sufficient for that enterprise, both for yourself and such company as ye will take with you, and present my heart to the Holy Sepulchre, whereas our Lord lay, seeing my body can not come there. And take with you such company and purveyance as shall be appertaining to your estate. And, wheresoever ye come, let it be known how ye carry with you the heart of King Robert of Scotland, at his instance and desire to be presented to the Holy Sepulchre." Then all the lords, that heard these words, wept for pity.

There, in the fifteenth century and early in the sixteenth, you have Malory and Berners writing beautiful English prose; prose the emotion of which (I dare to say) you must recognise if you have ears to hear. So you see that already our English prose not only achieves the "high moment," but seems to obey it rather and be lifted by it, until we ask ourselves, "Who could help writing nobly, having to tell how King Arthur died or how the Bruce?" Yes, but I bid you observe that Malory and Berners are both relating what, however noble, is quite simple, quite straightforward. It is when prose attempts to *philosophise*, to *express thoughts* as well as to relate simple sayings and doings—it is then *that* the trouble begins. When Malory has to philosophise death, to *think* about it, this is as far as he attains:—

"Ah, Sir Lancelot," said he, "thou wert head of all Christian Knights! And now I dare say," said Sir Ector, "that, Sir Lancelot, there thou liest, thou were never matched of none earthly hands; and thou were the curtiest knight that ever bare shield: and thou were the truest friend to thy lover that ever strood horse, and thou were the truest lover of a sinful man that ever loved woman; and thou were the kindest man that ever strooke with sword; and thou were the goodliest person that ever came among press of knights; and thou were the meekest man and gentlest that ever sat in hall among ladies; and thou were the sternest Knight to thy mortal foe that ever put spear in the rest."

Beautiful again, I grant! But note you that, eloquent as he can be on the virtues of his dead friend, when Sir Ector comes to the thought of death itself all he can accomplish is, "And now I dare say that, Sir Lancelot, there thou liest."

Let us make a leap in time and contrast this with Tyndale and the translators of our Bible, how they are able to make St. Paul speak of death:—

> So when this corruptible shall have put on incorruption, and this mortal shall have put on immortality, then shall be brought to pass the saying that is written, Death is swallowed up in victory. O death, where is thy sting? O grave, where is thy victory?

There you have something clean beyond what Malory or Berners could compass: there you have a different kind of high moment—a high moment of philosophising: there you have emotion impregnated with thought. It was necessary that our English verse even after Chaucer, our English prose after Malory and Berners, should overcome this most difficult gap (which stands for a real intellectual difference) if it aspired to be what to-day it is—a language of the first class, comparable with Greek and certainly no whit inferior to Latin or French.

. . . . .

Let us leave prose for a moment, and see how Verse threw its bridge over the gap. If you would hear the note of Chaucer at its deepest, you will find it in the famous exquisite lines of the Prioress' Prologue:—

> O moder mayde! O maydë moder fre!
> O bush unbrent, brenning in Moyses' sight!

in the complaint of Troilus, in the rapture of Griselda restored to her children:—

> O tendre, O dere, O yongë children myne,
> Your woful moder wendë stedfastly
> That cruel houndës or some foul vermyne
> Hadde eten you; but God of his mercy
> And your benignë fader tendrely
> Hath doon you kept. . . .

You will find a note quite as sincere in many a carol, many a ballad, of that time:—

> He came al so still
> There his mother was,
> As dew in April
> That falleth on the grass.

He came al so still
  To his mother's bour,
As dew in April
  That falleth on the flour.

He came al so still
  There his mother lay,
As dew in April
  That falleth on the spray.

Mother and maiden
  Was never none but she;
Well may such a lady
  Goddes mother be.

You get the most emotional note of the Ballad in such a stanza as this, from *The Nut-Brown Maid:—*

Though it be sung of old and young
  That I should be to blame,
Theirs be the charge that speak so large
  In hurting of my name;
For I will prove that faithful love
  It is devoid of shame;
In your distress and heaviness
  To part with you the same:
And sure all tho that do not so
  True lovers are they none:
For, in my mind, of all mankind
  I love but you alone.

All these notes, again, you will admit to be exquisite: but they gush straight from the unsophisticated heart: they are nowise deep save in innocent emotion: they are not *thoughtful.* So when Barbour breaks out in praise of Freedom, he cries

> A! Fredome is a noble thing!

And that is really as far as he gets. He goes on

> Fredome mayse man to hafe liking.

(Freedom makes man to choose what he likes; that is, makes him free)

> Fredome all solace to man giffis,
> He livis at ese that frely livis!
> A noble hart may haif nane ese,
> Na ellys nocht that may him plese,
> Gif fredome fail'th: for fre liking
> Is yharnit ouer all othir thing. . . .

—and so on for many lines; all saying the same thing, that man yearns for Freedom and is glad when he gets it, because then he is free; all hammering out the same observed fact, but all knocking vainly on the door of thought, which never opens to explain what Freedom *is.*

Now let us take a leap as we did with prose, and "taking off" from the Nut-Brown Maid's artless confession,

> in my mind, of all mankind
> I love but you alone,

let us alight on a sonnet of Shakespeare's—

Thy bosom is endearèd with all hearts
  Which I by lacking have supposèd dead:
And there reigns Love, and all Love's loving parts,
  And all those friends which I thought burièd.
How many a holy and obsequious tear
  Hath dear religious love stolen from mine eye
As interest of the dead!—which now appear
  But things removed, that hidden in thee lie.
Thou art the grave where buried love doth live,
  Hung with the trophies of my lovers gone,
Who all their parts of me to thee did give;
  —That due of many now is thine alone:
    Their images I loved I view in thee,
    And thou, all they, hast all the all of me.

What a new way of talking about love! Not a happier way—there is less of heart's-ease in these doubts, delicacies, subtleties—but how much more thoughtful! How has our Nut-Brown Maid eaten of the tree of knowledge!

Well, there happened a Shakespeare, to do this for English Verse: and Shakespeare was a miracle which I cheerfully leave others to rationalise for you, having, for my own part and so far as I have fared in life, found more profit in a capacity for simple wonder.

But I can tell you how the path was made straight to that miracle. The shock of the New

Learning upon Europe awoke men and unsealed men's eyes—unsealed the eyes of Englishmen in particular—to discover a literature, and the finest in the world, which *habitually philosophised life:* a literature which, whether in a chorus of Sophocles or a talk reported by Plato, or in a ribald page of Aristophanes or in a knotty chapter of Thucydides, was in one guise or another for ever asking *Why?* "What is man doing here, and *why* is he doing it?" "What is his purpose? his destiny?" "How stands he towards those unseen powers—call them the gods, or whatever you will—that guide and thwart, provoke, madden, control him so mysteriously?" "What are these things we call good and evil, life, love, death?"

These are questions which, once raised, haunt Man until he finds an answer—some sort of answer to satisfy him. Englishmen, hitherto content with the Church's answers but now aware of this great literature which answered so differently—and having other reasons to suspect what the Church said and did—grew aware that their literature had been as a child at play. It had never philosophised good and evil, life, love, or death: it had no literary forms for doing this; it had not even the vocabulary. So our ancestors saw that to catch up their lee-way—to make their report worthy of this wonderful, alluring discovery—new literary forms had to be invented—new, that is, in English: the sonnet, the drama, the verse in which the actors were to declaim, the essay, the invented tale. Then, for the vocabulary, obviously our fathers had either to go to Greek, which had invented the A. B. C. of philosophising; or to seek in the other languages which were already ahead of English in adapting that alphabet; or to give our English words new contents, new connotations, new meanings; or lastly, to do all three together.

Well, it was done; and in verse very fortunately done; thanks of course to many men, but thanks to two especially—to Sir Thomas Wyat, who led our poets to Italy, to study and adopt the forms in which Italy had cast its classical heritage; and to Marlowe, who impressed blank verse upon the drama. Of Marlowe I shall say nothing; for with what he achieved you are familiar enough. Of Wyat I may speak at length to you, one of these days; but here, to prepare you for what I hope then to prove—that Wyat is one of the heroes of our literature—I will give you three brief reasons why we should honour his memory:—

(1) He led the way. On the value of that service I shall content myself with quoting a passage from Newman:—

When a language has been cultivated in any particular department of thought, and so far as it has been generally perfected, an existing want has been supplied, and there is no need for further workmen. In its earliest times, while it is yet unformed, to write in it at all is almost a work of genius. It is like crossing a country before roads are made communicating between place and place. The authors of that age deserve to be Classics both because of what they do and because they can do it. It requires the courage and force of great talent to compose in the language at all; and the composition, when effected, makes a permanent impression on it.

This Wyat did. He was a pioneer and opened up a new country to Englishmen. But he did more.

(2) Secondly, he had the instinct to perceive that the lyric, if it would philosophise life, love, and the rest, must boldly introduce the personal note: since in fact when man asks questions about his fortune or destiny he asks them most effectively in the first person. "What am *I* doing? Why are *we* mortal? Why do *I* love *thee?*"

This again Wyat did: and again he did more.

For (3) thirdly—and because of this I am surest of his genius—again and again, using new thoughts in unfamiliar forms, he wrought out the result in language so direct, economical, natural, easy, that I know to this day no one who can better

Wyat's best in combining straight speech with melodious cadence. Take the lines *Is it possible?*—

Is it possible?
For to turn so oft;
To bring that lowest that was most aloft:
And to fall highest, yet to light soft?
Is it possible?

All is possible!
Whoso list believe;
Trust therefore first, and after preve;
As men wed ladies by licence and leave,
All is possible!

or again—

Forget not! O forget not this!—
How long ago hath been, and is,
The mind that never meant amiss:
Forget not yet!

or again (can personal note go straighter?)—

And wilt thou leave me thus?
Say nay, say nay, for shame!
—To save thee from the blame
Of all my grief and grame.
And wilt thou leave me thus?
Say nay! say nay![1]

[1] Say "nay," say "nay"; and *don't* say, "the answer is in the negative."

No: I have yet to mention the straightest, most natural of them all, and will read it to you in full—

What should I say?
  —Since Faith is dead
And Truth away
  From you is fled?
  Should I be led
    With doubleness?
    Nay! nay! mistress.

I promised you
  And you promised me
To be as true
  As I would be:
  But since I see
    You double heart,
    Farewell my part!

Thought for to take
  Is not my mind;
But to forsake
  One so unkind;
  And as I find,
    So will I trust,
    Farewell, unjust!

Can ye say nay
  But that you said
That I alway
  Should be obeyed?
  And—thus betrayed
    Or that I wist!
    Farewell, unkist!

I observe it noted on p. 190 of Volume III of *The Cambridge History of English Literature* that Wyat "was a pioneer and perfection was not to be expected of him. He has been described as a man stumbling over obstacles, continually falling but always pressing forward." I know not to what wiseacre we owe that pronouncement: but what do you think of it, after the lyric I have just quoted? I observe, further, on p. 26 of the same volume of the same work, that the Rev. T. M. Lindsay, D.D., Principal of the Glasgow College of the United Free Church of Scotland, informs us of Wilson's *Arte of Rhetorique* that

> there is little or no originality in the volume, save, perhaps, the author's condemnation of the use of French and Italian phrases and idioms, which he complains are "counterfeiting the kinges Englishe." The warnings of Wilson will not seem untimely if it be remembered that the earlier English poets of the period—Sir Thomas Wyatt the elder, and the Earl of Surrey—drew their inspiration from Petrarch and Ariosto, that their earliest attempts at poetry were translations from Italian sonnets, and that their maturer efforts were imitations of the sweet and stately measures and style of Italian poesie. The polish which men like Wyatt and Surrey were praised for giving to our "rude and homely manner of vulgar poesie" might have led to some degeneration.

Might it, indeed? As another Dominie would have said, "Pro-digious."[1]

But I have lingered too long with this favourite poet of mine and left myself room only to hand you the thread by following which you will come to the melodious philosophising of Shakespeare's Sonnets—

> Let me not to the marriage of true Minds
> Admit impediment. Love is not love
> Which alters where it alteration finds
> Or bends with the remover to remove.

Note the Latin words "impediment," "alteration," "remove." We are using the language of philosophy here or, rather, the "universal language," which had taken over the legacy of Greek. You may trace the use of it growing as, for example, you trace it through the Elizabethan song-books: and then (as I said) comes Shakespeare, and with Shakespeare the miracle.

The education of Prose was more difficult, and went through more violent convulsions. I suppose that the most of us—if, after reading a quantity of

[1] Thought for to take
Is not my mind;
But to forsake
This Principal of the Glasgow College of the United Free Church of Scotland—
Farewell, unkiss'd!

Elizabethan prose, we had the courage to tell plain truth, undaunted by the name of a great epoch—would confess to finding the mass of it clotted in sense as well as unmusical in sound, a disappointment almost intolerable after the simple melodious clarity of Malory and Berners. I, at any rate, must own that the most of Elizabethan prose pleases me little; and I speak not of Elizabethan prose at its worst, of such stuff as disgraced the already disgraceful Martin Marprelate Controversy, but of such as a really ingenious and ingenuous man like Thomas Nashe could write at his average. For a sample:—

> English Seneca read by candle-light yields many good sentences such as "Blood is a beggar" and so forth; and if you entreat him fair on a frosty morning, he will afford you whole Hamlets, I should say handfuls of tragical speeches. . . . Sufficeth them [that is, modern followers of Seneca] to bodge up a blank verse with if's and and's, and others, while for recreation after their candle-stuff having starched their beards most curiously, to make a peripatetical path into the inner parts of the city, and spend two or three hours in turning over the French *Doudie*, where they attract more infection in one minute than they can do eloquence all the days of their life by conversing with any authors of like argument.

This may be worth studying historically, to understand the difficulties our prose had to encounter and overcome. But no one would seriously propose it as a model for those who would write well, which is our present business. I have called it "clotted." It is, to use a word of the time, "farced" with conceits; it needs straining.

Its one merit consists in this, that it is struggling, fumbling, to say something: that is, to *make* something. It is not, like modern jargon, trying to dodge something. English prose, in short, just here is passing through a period of puberty, of green sickness: and, looking at it historically, we may own that its throes are commensurate with the stature of the grown man to be.

These throes tear it every way. On the one hand we have Ascham, pedantically enough, apologising that he writes in the English tongue (yet with a sure instinct he does it):

> If any man would blame me, either for taking such a matter in hand, or else for writing it in the English tongue, this answer I may make him, that what the best of the realm think it honest for them to use, I, one of the meanest sort, ought not to suppose it vile for me to write. . . . And as for the Latin or Greek tongue, everything is so excellently done in them that none can do better. In the English tongue, contrary, everything in a manner so meanly, both for the matter and the handling, that no man can do worse.

On the other hand you have euphuism with its antithetical tricks and poises, taking all prose by storm for a time: euphuism, to be revived two hundred years later, and find a new avatar in the Johnsonian balance; euphuism, dead now, yet alive enough in its day.

For all these writers were alive: and I tell you it is an inspiriting thing to be alive and trying to write English. All these authors were alive and trying to *do* something. Unconsciously for the most part they were striving to philosophise the vocabulary of English prose and find a rhythm for its periods.

And then, as already had happened to our verse, to our prose too there befel a miracle.

You will not ask me "What miracle?" I mean, of course, the Authorised Version of the Bible.

I grant you, to be sure, that the path to the Authorised Version was made straight by previous translators, notably by William Tyndale. I grant you that Tyndale was a man of genius, and Wyclif before him a man of genius. I grant you that the forty-seven men who produced the Authorised Version worked in the main upon Tyndale's version, taking that for their basis. Nay, if you choose to say that Tyndale was a miracle in himself, I cheerfully grant you that as well. But, in a lecture one must not multiply miracles *praeter necessitatem;* and when Tyndale has been granted you have yet to face the miracle that forty-seven men—not one of them known, outside of this performance, for any superlative talent—sat in committee and almost consistently, over a vast extent of work—improved upon what Genius had done. I give you the word of an old committee-man that this is not the way of committees—that only by miracle is it the way of any committee. Doubtless the forty-seven were all good men and godly: but doubtless also good and godly were the Dean and Chapter who dealt with Alfred Steven's tomb of the Duke of Wellington in St. Paul's Cathedral; and you know what *they* did. Individual genius such as Tyndale's or even Shakespeare's, though we cannot explain it, we may admit as occurring somehow, and not incredibly, in the course of nature. But that a large committee of forty-seven should have gone steadily through the great mass of Holy Writ, seldom interfering with genius, yet, when interfering, seldom missing to improve: that a committee of forty-seven should have captured (or even, let us say, should have retained and improved) a rhythm so personal, so constant, that our Bible has the voice of one author speaking through its many mouths: that, Gentlemen, is a wonder before which I can only stand humble and aghast.

Does it or does it not strike you as queer that the people who set you "courses of study" in English Literature never include the Authorised Version, which not only intrinsically but historically is out and away the greatest book of English Prose. Perhaps they pay you the silent compliment of supposing that you are perfectly acquainted with it? . . . I wonder. It seems as if they thought the Martin Marprelate Controversy, for example, more important somehow.

"So when this corruptible shall have put on incorruption, and this mortal shall have put on immortality. . ."

"Many waters cannot quench love, neither can the floods drown it: if a man would give all the substance of his house for love, it would utterly be contemned."

"The king's daughter is all glorious within: her clothing is of wrought gold."

"Thine eyes shall see the King in his beauty: they shall behold the land that is very far off."

"And a man shall be as an hiding-place from the wind, and a covert from the tempest; as rivers of water in a dry place, as the shadow of a great rock in a weary land."

When a nation has achieved this manner of diction, those rhythms for its dearest beliefs, a literature is surely established. Just there I find the effective miracle, making the blind to see, the lame to leap. Wyclif, Tyndale, Coverdale, and others before the forty-seven had wrought. The Authorised Version, setting a seal on all, set a seal on our national style, thinking and speaking. It has cadences homely and sublime, yet so harmonises them that the voice is always one. Simple men—holy and humble men of heart like Isaak Walton or Bunyan —have their lips touched and speak to the homelier tune. Proud men, scholars,—Milton, Sir Thomas Browne—practice the rolling Latin sentence; but upon the rhythms of our Bible they, too, fall back. "The great mutations of the world are acted, or time may be too short for our designs." "Acquaint thyself with the Choragium of the stars." "There is nothing immortal but immortality." The precise man Addison cannot excel one parable in brevity or in heavenly clarity: the two parts of Johnson's antithesis come to no more than this, "Our Lord has gone up to the sound of a trump: with the sound of a trump our Lord has gone up." The Bible controls its enemy Gibbon as surely as it haunts the curious music of a light sentence of Thackeray's. It is in everything we see, hear, feel, because it is in us, in our blood.

What madman, then, will say "Thus or thus far shalt thou go" to a prose thus invented and thus with its free rhythms, after three hundred years, working on the imagination of Englishmen? Or who shall determine its range, whether of thought or of music? You have received it by inheritance, Gentlemen: it is yours, freely yours—to direct your words through life as well as your hearts.

VII

Some Principles Reaffirmed

LET me begin to-day, Gentlemen, with a foot-note to my last lecture. It ended, as you may remember, upon an earnest appeal to you, if you would write good English, to study the Authorised Version of the Scriptures; to learn from it, moreover, how by mastering *rhythm*, our Prose overcame the capital difficulty of Prose and attuned itself to rival its twin instrument, Verse; compassing almost equally with Verse man's thought however sublime, his emotion however profound.

Now in the course of my remarks I happened—maybe a little incautiously—to call the Authorised Version a "miracle"; using that word in a colloquial sense, in which no doubt you accepted it; meaning no more than that the thing passed my understanding. I have allowed that the famous forty-seven owed an immense deal to earlier translators—to the Bishops, to Tyndale, to the Wyclif Version, as themselves allowed it eagerly in their preface:—

Truly (good Christian reader) wee never thought from the beginning that we should needs to make a new Translation, nor yet to make of a bad one a good one . . . but to make a good one better, or out of many good ones one principall good one, not justly to be excepted against: that hath bene our indeavour, that our marke.[1]

Nevertheless the Authorised Version astounds me, as I believe it will astound you when you compare it with earlier translations. Aristotle (it has been said) invented Chance to cover the astonishing fact that there were certain phenomena for which he found himself wholly unable to account. Just so, if one may compare very small things with very great, I spoke of the Authorised Version as a "miracle." It was, it remains, marvellous to me.

Should these deciduous discourses ever come to be pressed within the leaves of a book, I believe their general meaning will be as clear to readers as I hope it is to you who give me so much pleasure by pursuing them—almost (shall I say?) like Wordsworth's Kitten with those other falling leaves:—

That almost I could repine
That your transports are not mine.

[1] See note at the end of this Lecture.

But meanwhile certain writers in the newspapers are assuming that by this word "miracle" I meant to suggest to you a something like plenary inspiration in these forty-seven men; an inspiration at once supernatural and so authoritative that it were sacrilege now to alter their text by one jot or tittle.

Believe me, I intended nothing of the sort: for that, in my plain opinion, would be to make a fetish of the book. One of these days I hope to discuss with you what inspiration is: with what accuracy—with what meaning, if any—we can say of a poet that he is inspired; questions which have puzzled many wise men from Plato downwards.

But certainly I never dreamt of claiming plenary inspiration for the forty-seven. Nay, if you will have it, they now and again wrote stark nonsense. Remember that I used this very same word "miracle" of Shakespeare, meaning again that the total Shakespeare quite outpasses my comprehension; yet Shakespeare, too, on occasion talks stark nonsense, or at any rate stark bombast. He never blotted a line—"I would he had blotted a thousand," says Ben Jonson: and Ben Jonson was right. Shakespeare could have blotted out two or three thousand lines: he was great enough to afford it. Somewhere Matthew Arnold supposes us as challenging Shakespeare over this and that weak or bombastic passage, and Shakespeare answering with his tolerant smile, that no doubt we were right, but after all, "Did it greatly matter?"

So we offer no real derogation to the forty-seven in asserting that here and there they wrote nonsense. They could afford it. But we do stultify criticism if, adoring the grand total of wisdom and beauty, we prostrate ourselves indiscriminately before what is good and what is bad, what is sublime sense and what is nonsense, and forbid any reviser to put forth a hand to the ark.

The most of us Christians go to church on Christmas Day, and there we listen to this from Isaiah, chapter ix, verses 1–7:—

> Nevertheless the dimness shall not be such as was in her vexation, when at the first he lightly afflicted the land of Zebulun and the land of Naphtali, and afterward did more grievously afflict her by the way of the sea, beyond Jordan, in Galilee of the nations.
>
> The people that walked in darkness have seen a great light: they that dwell in the land of the shadow of death, upon them hath the light shined.
>
> Thou hast multiplied the nation, and not increased the joy: they joy before thee according to the joy in harvest, and as men rejoice when they divide the spoil.

For thou hast broken the yoke of his burden, and the staff of his shoulder, the rod of his oppressor, as in the day of Midian.

For every battle of the warrior is with confused noise, and garments rolled in blood: but this shall be with burning and fuel of fire.

For unto us a child is born, unto us a son is given.

The forty-seven keep their majestic rhythm. But have you ever, sitting in church on a Christmas morning, asked yourself what it all means, or if it mean anything more than a sing-song according somehow with the holly and ivy around the pillars? "*Thou hast multiplied the nation, and not increased the joy: they joy before thee according to the joy in harvest.*" But why—if the joy be not increased? "*For every battle of the warrior is with confused noise, and garments rolled in blood: but this shall be with burning and fuel of fire.*" Granted the rhythmical antithesis, where is the real antithesis, the difference, the improvement? If a battle there must be, how is burning better than garments rolled in blood? And, in fine, what is it all about? Now let us turn to the Revised Version:—

But there shall be no gloom to her that was in anguish. In the former time he brought into contempt the land of Zebulun and the land of Naphtali, but in the latter time hath he made it glorious, by the way of the sea, beyond Jordan, Galilee of the nations.

The people that walked in darkness have seen a great light: they that dwelt in the land of the shadow of death, upon them hath the light shined. Thou hast multiplied the nation, thou *hast* increased their joy: they joy before thee according to the joy in harvest, as men rejoice when they divide the spoil.

For the yoke of his burden, and the staff of his shoulder, the rod of his oppressor, thou hast broken as in the day of Midian.

For all the armour of the armed man in the tumult, and the garments rolled in blood, shall even be for burning, for fuel of fire.

For unto us a child is born, unto us a son is given; and the government shall be upon his shoulder: and his name shall be called Wonderful, Counsellor, Mighty God, Everlasting Father, Prince of Peace.

I say (knowing no Hebrew, merely assuming our Revisers to be at least no worse scholars than the forty-seven) that here, with the old cadences kept so far as possible, we are given sense in place of nonsense: and I ask you to come to the Revised Version with a fair mind. I myself came to it with some prejudice; in complete ignorance of Hebrew, and with no more than the usual amount of Hellenistic Greek. I grant at once that the Revised New Testament was a literary fiasco; largely due (if gossip may be trusted) to trouble with the Greek Aorist, and an unwise decision—in my opinion the most gratuitously unwise a translator can take—to use one and the same English word, always and in every connotation, as representing one and the same Greek word: for in any two languages few words are precisely equivalent. A fiasco at any rate the Revised New Testament was, deserving in a dozen ways and in a thousand passages the scorn which Professor Saintsbury has recently heaped on it. But I protest against the injustice of treating the two Revisions—of the New Testament and of the Old—as a single work, and saddling the whole with the sins of a part. For two years I spent half-an-hour daily in reading the Authorised and Revised Versions side by side, marking as I went, and in this way worked through the whole—Old Testament, Apocrypha, New Testament. I came to it (as I have said) with some prejudice; but I closed the books on a conviction, which my notes sustain for me, that the Revisers of the Old Testament performed their task delicately, scrupulously, on the whole with great good judgment; that the critic does a wrong who brings them under his indiscriminate censure; that on the whole they have clarified the sense of the Authorised Version while respecting its consecrated rhythms; and that—to name an example, that you may test my words and judge for yourselves—the solemn splendour of that most wonderful poem, the story of Job, διαλάμπει, "shines through" the new translation as it never shone through the old.

. . . .

And now, Gentlemen (as George Herbert said on a famous occasion), let us tune our instruments.

Before discussing with you another and highly important question of style in writing, I will ask you to look back for a few moments on the road we have travelled.

We have agreed that our writing should be *appropriate:* that it should fit the occasion; that it should rise and fall with the subject, be grave where that is serious, where it is light not afraid of what Stevenson in *The Wrong Box* calls "a little judicious levity." If your writing observe these precepts, it will be well-mannered writing.

To be sure, much in addition will depend on yourself—on what you are or have made yourself, since in writing the style can never be separated from the man. But neither can it in the practice of virtue: yet, though men differ in character, I do not observe that moralists forbear from laying down general rules of excellence. Now if you will recall our further conclusion, that writing to be good must be persuasive (since persuasion is the only true intellectual process), and will test this by a passage of Newman's I am presently to quote to you, from his famous "definition of a gentleman,". I think you will guess pretty accurately the general law of excellence I would have you, as Cambridge men, tribally and particularly obey.

Newman says of a gentleman that among other things:

> He is never mean or little in his disputes, never takes unfair advantage, never mistakes personalities or sharp sayings for arguments, or insinuates evil which he dare not say out. . . . If he engages in controversy of any kind, his disciplined intellect preserves him from the blundering discourtesy of better perhaps, but less educated minds; who, like blunt weapons, tear and hack instead of cutting clean, who mistake the point in argument, waste their strength on trifles, misconceive their adversary, and leave the question more involved than they found it. He may be right or wrong in his opinion: but he is too clear-sighted to be unjust. He is simple as he is forcible, and as brief as he is decisive.

Enough for the moment on this subject: but commit these words to your hearts, and you will not only triumph in newspaper controversy. You will do better: you will avoid it.

To proceed.—We found further that our writing should be *accurate:* because language expresses thought—is, indeed, the only expression of thought—and if we lack the skill to speak precisely, our thought will remain confused, ill-defined. The editor of a mining paper in Denver, U. S. A., boldly the other day laid down this law, that niceties of language were mere "frills"; all a man needed was to "get there," that is, to say what he wished in his own way. But just here, we found, lies the mischief. You will not get there by hammering away on your own untutored impulse. You must first be your own reader, chiselling out the thought definitely for yourself: and, after that, must carve out the intaglio yet more sharply and neatly, if you would impress its image accurately upon the wax of other men's minds. We found that even for Men of Science this neat clean carving of words was a very necessary accomplishment. As Sir James Barrie once observed, "The Man of Science appears to be the only man who has something to say, just now—and the only man who does not know how to say it." But the trouble by no means ends with science. Our poets—those gifted strangely prehensile men who, as I said in my first lecture, seem to be born with filaments by which they apprehend, and along which they conduct, the half-secrets of life to us ordinary mortals—our poets would appear to be scamping artistic labour, neglecting to reduce the vague impressions to the clearly cut image which is, after all, what helps. It may be a triumph that they have taught modern French poetry to be suggestive. I think it would be more profitable could they learn from France—that nation of fine workmen—to be definite.

But about "getting there"—I ask you to remember Wolfe, with the seal of his fate on him, stepping into his bateau on the dark St. Lawrence River and quoting as they tided him over:—

> The boast of heraldry, the pomp of power,
>   And all that beauty, all that wealth e'er gave,
> Await alike th' inevitable hour;
>   The paths of glory lead but to the grave.

"I had rather have written those lines," said Wolfe, "than conquer Canada." That is how our forefathers valued noble writing. The Denver editor holds that you may write as you please so long as you get there. Well, Wolfe got there: and so, in Wolfe's opinion, did Gray: but perhaps to Wolfe and Gray, and to the Denver editor, "there" happened to mean two different places. Wolfe got to the Heights of Abraham.

Further, it was against this loose adaptation of

words to thought and to things that we protested in our interpolated lecture on Jargon, which is not so much bad writing as the avoidance of writing. The man who employs jargon does not get "there" at all, even in a raw rough pioneering fashion: he just walks around "there" in the ambient tracks of others. Let me fly as high as I can and quote you two recent achievements by Cabinet Ministers, as reported in the Press:—(1) "Mr. McKenna's reasons for releasing from Holloway Prison Miss Lenton while on remand charged *in connexion with* (sweet phrase!) the firing of the tea pavilion in Kew Gardens are given in a letter which he has *caused to be forwarded* to a correspondent who inquired *as to* the circumstances of the release. The letter says, 'I am desired by the Home Secretary to say that Lilian Lenton was reported by the medical officer at Holloway Prison to be in a state of collapse and in imminent danger of death *consequent upon* her refusal to take food. Three courses were open—(1) To leave her to die; (2) To attempt to feed her forcibly, which the medical officer advised would probably entail death in her existing condition: (3) To release her. The Home Secretary adopted the last course.'"

"Would probably entail death in her existing condition"! Will anyone tell me how Mr.

McKenna or anyone else could kill, or (as he prefers to put it) entail death upon, Miss Lenton in a non-existing condition?

(2) Next take the Chancellor of the Exchequer. As we know, the Chancellor of the Exchequer can use incisive speech when he chooses. On May 8th, as reported in next day's *Morning Post*, Mr. Lloyd George, answering a question, delivered himself of this to an attentive Senate:—

> With regard to Mr. Noel Buxton's questions, I cannot answer for an enquiry which is *of a private and confidential character*, for although I am *associated with it* I am not associated with it as a Minister of the Crown. . . . Those enquiries are *of a very careful systematic and scientific character*, and are being conducted by the ablest investigators in this country, some of whom have reputations *of international character*. I am glad to think that the investigation is *of a most impartial character*.

It must be a comforting thought, that an inquiry of a private and confidential character is also of a very systematic and scientific character, and besides being of a most impartial character, is conducted by men of international character—whatever that may happen to mean. What *is* an international character, and what would you give for one?

We found that this way of talking, while pretending to be something pontifical, is really not prose at all, nor reputable speech at all, but jargon; nor is the offence to be excused by pleading, as I have heard it pleaded, that Mr. Lloyd George was not using his own phraseology but quoting from a paper supplied him by some permanent official of the Treasury: since we select our civil servants among men of decent education and their salaries warrant our stipulating that they shall be able, at least, to speak and write their mother tongue.

We laid down certain rules to help us in the way of straight Prose:—

(1) *Almost always prefer the concrete word to the abstract.*

(2) *Almost always prefer the direct word to the circumlocution.*

(3) *Generally use transitive verbs, that strike their object; and use them in the active voice, eschewing the stationary passive, with its little auxiliary* its's *and* was's, *and its participles getting into the light of your adjectives, which should be few. For, as a rough law, by his use of the straight verb and by his economy of adjectives you can tell a man's style, if it be masculine or neuter, writing or "composition."*

The authors of that capital handbook *The*

King's English, which I have already recommended to you, add two rules:—

(4) *Prefer the short word to the long.*

(5) *Prefer the Saxon word to the Romance.*

But these two precepts you would have to modify by so long a string of exceptions that I do not commend them to you. In fact I think them false in theory and likely to be fatal in practice. For, as my last lecture tried to show, you no sooner begin to philosophise things instead of merely telling a tale of them than you must go to the Mediterranean languages: because in these man first learnt to discuss his "why" and "how," and these languages yet guard the vocabulary.

Lastly we saw how, by experimenting with rhythm, our prose "broke its birth's invidious bar" and learnt to scale the forbidden heights.

Now by attending to the few plain rules given above you may train yourselves to write sound, straightforward, work-a-day English. But if you would write melodious English, I fear the gods will require of you what they ought to have given you at birth—something of an ear. Yet the most of us have ears, of sorts; and I believe that, though we can only acquire it by assiduous practice, the most of us can wonderfully improve our talent of the ear.

If you will possess yourselves of a copy of Quintilian, or borrow one from any library (Bohn's translation will do) and turn to his 9th book, you will find a hundred ways indicated, illustrated, classified, in which a writer or speaker can vary his style, modulate it, lift or depress it, regulate its balance.

All these rules, separately worth studying, if taken together may easily bewilder and dishearten you. Let me choose just two, and try to hearten you by showing that, even with these two only, you can go a long way.

Take the use of right emphasis. What Quintilian says of right emphasis—or the most important thing he says—is this:—

> There is sometimes an extraordinary force in some particular word, which, if it be placed in no very conspicuous position in the middle part of a sentence, is likely to escape the attention of the hearer and to be obscured by the words surrounding it; but if it be put at the end of the sentence is urged upon the reader's sense and imprinted on his mind.

That seems obvious enough, for English use as well as for Latin. "The wages of sin is Death"—anyone can see how much more emphatic that is than "Death is the wages of sin." But let your minds work on this matter of emphasis, and discover how emphasis has always its right point somewhere, though it be not at all necessarily at the end of the sentence. Take a sentence in which the strong words actually repeat themselves for emphasis:—

> Babylon is fallen, is fallen, that great city.

Our first impulse would be to place the emphasis at the end:—

> Babylon, that great city, is fallen, is fallen.

The Latin puts it at the beginning:—

> Cecidit, cecidit, Babylonia illa magna.
> Fallen, fallen, is Babylon, that great city.

The forty-seven preserved the "falling close" so exquisite in the Latin; the emphasis, already secured by repetition, they accentuated by lengthening the pause. I would urge on you that in every sentence there is just a right point of emphasis which you must train your ears to detect. So your writing will acquire not only emphasis, but balance, and you will instinctively avoid such an ill-emphasised sentence as this, which, not naming the author, I will quote for your delectation:—

> "Are Japanese Aprils always as lovely as this?" asked the man in the light tweed suit of two others in

immaculate flannels with crimson sashes round their waists and puggarees folded in cunning plaits round their broad Terai hats.

Explore, next, what (though critics have strangely neglected it) to my mind stands the first, or almost the first, secret of beautiful writing in English, whether in prose or in verse; I mean that inter-play of vowel-sounds in which no language can match us. We have so many vowel sounds indeed, and so few vowels to express them, that the foreigner, mistaking our modesty, complains against God's plenty. We alone, for example, sound by a natural vowel that noble *I*, which other nations can only compass by diphthongs. Let us consider that vowel for a moment or two and mark how it leads off the dance of the Graces, its sisters:—

> Arise, shine, for thy light is come, and the glory of the Lord is risen upon thee.

Mark how expressively it drops to the solemn vowel "O," and anon how expressively it reasserts itself to express rearisen delight:—

> Arise, shine, for thy light is come, and the glory of the Lord is risen upon thee. For behold the darkness shall cover the earth, and gross darkness the people: but the Lord shall arise upon thee, and his glory shall

be seen upon thee. And the Gentiles shall come to thy light, and Kings to the brightness of thy rising.

Take another passage in which the first lift of this *I* vowel yields to its graver sisters as though the sound sank into the very heart of the sense.

I will arise and go to my father, and will say unto him, "Father, I have sinned against heaven and before thee, and am no more worthy to be called thy son."

"And am n*o* m*o*re w*o*rthy to be called thy s*o*n." Mark the deep O's. "For this my son was dead and is alive again; he was lost and is found." "O my son, my son Absalom"—observe the I and O how they interchime, until the O of sorrow tolls the lighter note down:—

O my son Absalom, my son, my son Absalom! Would God I had died for thee, O Absalom, my son, my son!

Or take this lyric, by admission one of the loveliest written in this present age, and mark here too how the vowels play and ring and chime and toll.

I will arise and go now, and go to Innisfree,
    And a small cabin build there, of clay and wattles
        made;

N*i*ne b*ea*n r*o*ws will I have there, a h*i*ve for the h*o*ney b*ee*,
And l*i*ve al*o*ne in a b*ee*-l*ou*d gl*a*de.[1]

And I shall have some peace there, for peace comes dropping slow,
Dropping from the veils of the morning to where the cricket sings;
There midnight's all a glimmer, and noon a purple glow,
And evening full of the linnet's wings.
I will arise and go now, for always night and day
I hear lake-water lapping, and low sounds by the shore;
While I stand on the roadway, or on the pavement grey,
I hear it in the deep heart's core.

I think if you will but open your ears to this beautiful vowel-play which runs through all the best of our prose and poetry, whether you ever learn to master it or not, you will have acquired a new delight, and one various enough to last you though you live to a very old age.

All this of which I am speaking is Art: and Literature being an Art, do you not see how personal a thing it is—how it cannot escape being

[1] I E O : I O E
Ĭ O : E OU A

"As m*u*sing sl*o*w *I* h*ai*l
Th*y* genial l*o*ved ret*u*rn."
COLLINS, *Ode to Evening*.

personal? No two men (unless they talk jargon) say the same thing in the same way. As is a man's imagination, as is his character, as is the harmony in himself, as is his ear, as is his skill, so and not otherwise he will speak, so and not otherwise than they can respond to that imagination, that character, that order of his intellect, that harmony of his soul, his hearers will hear him. Let me conclude with this great passage from Newman which I beg you, having heard it, to ponder:—

If then the power of speech is as great as any that can be named,—if the origin of language is by many philosophers considered nothing short of divine—if by means of words the secrets of the heart are brought to light, pain of soul is relieved, hidden grief is carried off, sympathy conveyed, experience recorded, and wisdom perpetuated,—if by great authors the many are drawn up into unity, national character is fixed, a people speaks, the past and the future, the East and the West are brought into communication with each other,—if such men are, in a word, the spokesmen and prophets of the human family—it will not answer to make light of Literature or to neglect its study: rather we may be sure that, in proportion as we master it in whatever language, and imbibe its spirit, we shall ourselves become in our own measure the ministers of like benefits to others—be they many or few, be they in the obscurer or the more distinguished walks of life—who are united to us by social ties, and are within the sphere of our personal influence.

Note on page 154.

I append the following specimen translations of the famous passage in St. Paul's *First Epistle to the Corinthians* xv. 51 sqq. I choose this because (1) it is an important passage; (2) it touches a high moment of philosophising; (3) the comparison seems to me to represent with great fairness to Tyndale the extent of the forty-seven's debt to him; (4) it shows that they meant exactly what they said in their Preface; and (5) it illustrates, towards the close, their genius for improvement. The Greek runs:—

'Ιδοὺ μυστήριον ὑμῖν λέγω· Πάντες μὲν οὐ κοιμηθησόμεθα· πάντες δὲ ἀλλαγησόμεθα, ἐν ἀτόμῳ, ἐν ῥιπῇ ὀφθαλμοῦ, ἐν τῇ ἐσχάτῃ σάλπιγγι· σαλπίσει γάρ, καὶ οἱ νεκροὶ ἐγερθήσονται ἄφθαρτοι, καὶ ἡμεῖς ἀλλαγησόμεθα. δεῖ γὰρ τὸ φθαρτὸν τοῦτο ἐνδύσασθαι ἀφθαρσίαν, καὶ τὸ θνητὸν τοῦτο ἐνδύσασθαι ἀθανασίαν. ὅταν δὲ τὸ φθαρτὸν τοῦτο ἐνδύσηται ἀφθαρσίαν, καὶ τὸ θνητὸν τοῦτο ἐνδύσηται ἀθανασίαν, τότε γενήσεται ὁ λόγος ὁ γεγραμμένος, "Κατεπόθη ὁ θάνατος εἰς νῖκος." "Ποῦ σου, θάνατε, τὸ κέντρον; ποῦ σου, ᾅδη, τὸ νῖκος;"

Wyclif translates:—

Lo, I seie to you pryvyte of holi thingis | and alle we schulen rise agen | but not alle we schuln be chaungid | in a moment in the twynkelynge of an yë, in the last trumpe | for the trumpe schal sowne: and deed men schulen rise agen with out corrupcion, and we schuln be changid | for it bihoveth this corruptible thing to clothe uncorrupcion and this deedly thing to putte aweye undeedlynesse. But whanne this deedli thing schal clothe undeedlynesse | thanne schal the word be don that is written | deeth is sopun up in victorie | deeth, where is thi victorie? deeth, where is thi pricke?

Tyndale:—

Beholde I shewe you a mystery. We shall not all slepe: but we shall all be chaunged | and that in a moment | and in the twinclinge of an eye | at the sounde of the last trompe. For the trompe shall blowe, and the deed shall ryse incorruptible and we shalbe chaunged. For this corruptible must put on incorruptibilite: and this mortall must put on immortalite. When this corruptible hath put on incorruptibilite | and this mortall hath put on immortalite: then shalbe brought to pass the saying that is written. "Deeth is consumed in to victory." Deeth, where is thy stynge? Hell, where is thy victory?

The Authorised Version:—

Behold, I shew you a mystery; we shall not all sleepe, but wee shall all be changed, in a moment, in the twinckling of an eye, at the last trumpe, (for the trumpet shall sound, and the dead shall be raised incorruptible, and we shall be changed). For this corruptible must put on incorruption, and this mortall must put on immortalitie. So when this corruptible shall have put on incorruption and this mortall shall have put on immortality, then shall be brought to passe the saying that is written, "Death is swallowed up in victory." O Death, where is thy sting? O grave, where is thy victory?

VIII

On the Lineage of English Literature (I)

YOU may think it strange, Gentlemen, that out of a course of ten lectures which aim to treat English Literature as an affair of practice, I should propose to spend two in discussing our literary lineage: a man's lineage and geniture being reckoned, as a rule, among the things he cannot be reasonably asked to amend. But since of high breeding is begotten (as most of us believe) a disposition to high thoughts, high deeds; since to have it and be modestly conscious of it is to carry within us a faithful monitor persuading us to whatsoever in conduct is gentle, honourable, of good repute, and so silently dissuading us from base thoughts, low ends, ignoble gains; seeing, moreover, that a man will often do more to match his father's virtue than he would to improve himself; I shall endeavour, in this and my next lecture, to scour that spur of ancestry and present it to you as so bright and sharp an incentive that you, who read English Literature and practise writing here in Cambridge, shall not pass out from her insensible of the dignity of your studies, or without pride or remorse according, as you have interpreted in practice the motto, *Noblesse oblige.*

'Tis wisdom, and that high,
For men to use their fortune reverently
Even in youth.

Let me add that, just as a knowledge of his family failings will help one man in economising his estate, or warn another to shun for his health the pleasures of the table, so some knowledge of our lineage in letters may put us, as Englishmen, on the watch for certain national defects (for such we have), on our guard against certain sins which too easily beset us. Nay, this watchfulness may well reach down from matters of great moment to seeming trifles. It is good for us to recognise with Wordsworth that

We must be free or die, who speak the tongue
That Shakespeare spake; the faith and morals hold
Which Milton held. In everything we are sprung
Of Earth's first blood, have titles manifold.

But, though less important, it is good also to recognise that, as sons of Cambridge, we equally offend against her breeding when in our scientific writings we allow ourselves to talk of a microbe as an "antibody."

Now, because a great deal of what I have to say this morning, if not heretical, will yet run contrary to the vogue and practice of the Schools for these thirty years, I will take the leap into my subject over a greater man's back and ask you to listen with particular attention to the following long passage from a writer whose opinion you may challenge, but whose authority to speak as a master of English prose no one in this room will deny.

When (says Cardinal Newman) we survey the stream of human affairs for the last three thousand years, we find it to run thus:—At first sight there is so much fluctuation, agitation, ebbing and flowing, that we may despair to discern any law in its movements, taking the earth as its bed and mankind as its contents; but on looking more closely and attentively we shall discern, in spite of the heterogeneous materials and the various histories and fortunes which are found in the race of man during the long period I have mentioned, a certain formation amid the chaos—one and one only,—and extending, though not over the whole earth, yet through a very considerable portion of it. Man is a social being and can hardly exist without society, and in matter of fact societies have ever existed all over the habitable earth. The greater part of these associations have been political or religious, and have been comparatively limited in extent and temporary. They have been formed and dissolved by the force of accidents, or by inevitable circumstances; and when we have enumerated them one by one we have made of them all that can be made. But there is one remarkable association which attracts the attention of the philosopher, not political nor religious—or at least only partially and not essentially such—which began in the earliest times and grew with each succeeding age till it reached its complete development, and then continued on, vigorous and unwearied, and still remains as definite and as firm as ever it was. Its bond is *a common civilisation:* and though there are other civilisations in the world, as there are other societies, yet *this* civilisation, together with the society which is its creation and its home, is so distinctive and luminous in its character, so imperial in its extent, so imposing in its duration, and so utterly without rival on the face of the earth, that the association may fitly assume to itself the title of "Human Society," and *its* civilisation the abstract term "Civilisation."

There are indeed great outlying portions of mankind which are not, perhaps never have been, included in this Human Society; still they are outlying portions and nothing else, fragmentary, unsociable, solitary and unmeaning, protesting and revolting against the grand central formation of which I am speaking, but not uniting with each other into a second whole. I am not denying, of course, the civilisation of the Chinese, for instance, though it be not our civilisation; but it is a huge, stationary, unattractive, morose civilisation. Nor do I deny a civilisation to the Hindoos, nor to the ancient Mexicans, nor to the Saracens, nor (in a certain sense) to the Turks; but each of these races has its own civilisation, as separate from one another as from ours.

I do not see how they can be all brought under one idea. . . .

Gentlemen, let me here observe that I am not entering upon the question of races, or upon their history. I have nothing to do with ethnology, I take things as I find them on the surface of history and am but classifying phenomena. Looking, then, at the countries which surround the Mediterranean Sea as a whole, I see them to be from time immemorial, the seat of an association of intellect and mind such as to deserve to be called the Intellect and the Mind of the Human Kind. Starting as it does, and advancing from certain centres, till their respective influences intersect and conflict, and then at length intermingle and combine, a common Thought has been generated, and a common Civilisation defined and established. Egypt is one such starting point, Syria another, Greece a third, Italy a fourth and North Africa a fifth—afterwards France and Spain. As time goes on, and as colonisation and conquest work their changes, we see a great association of nations formed, of which the Roman Empire is the maturity and the most intelligible expression: an association, however, not political but mental, based on the same intellectual ideas and advancing by common intellectual methods. . . . In its earliest age it included far more of the Eastern world than it has since; in these later times it has taken into its compass a new hemisphere; in the Middle Ages it lost Africa, Egypt and Syria, and extended itself to Germany, Scandinavia and the British Isles. At one time its territory was flooded by strange and barbarous races, but the existing civilisation was vigorous enough to vivify what threatened to stifle it, and to assimilate to the old social forms what came to expel them: and thus the civilisation of modern times remains what it was of old; not Chinese, or Hindoo, or Mexican, or Saracen . . . but the lineal descendant, or rather the continuation—*mutatis mutandis*—of the civilisation which began in Palestine and Greece.

To omit, then, all minor debts such as what of arithmetic, what of astronomy, what of geography, we owe to the Saracen, from Palestine we derive the faith of Europe shared (in the language of the Bidding Prayer) by all Christian people dispersed throughout the world; as to Greece we owe the rudiments of our Western art, philosophy, letters; and not only the rudiments but the continuing inspiration, so that—though entirely superseded in worship, as even in the Athens of Pericles they were worshipped only by an easy, urbane, more than half humorous tolerance—Apollo and the Muses, Zeus and the great ones of Olympus, Hermes and Hephaestus, Athene in her armour, with her vanquisher the foam-born irresistible Aphrodite, these remain the authentic gods of our literature, beside whom the gods of northern Europe—Odin, Thor, Freya—are strangers, unhomely, uncanny as the shadows of unfamiliar furniture on the walls of an inn. Sprung though great numbers of us are from the loins of Northmen, it is in these gracious deities of the South that we find the familiar and the real, as from the heroes of the sister-island, Cucullain and Concobar, we turn to Hercules, to Perseus, to Bellerophon, even to actual men of history, saying, "Give us Leonidas, give us Horatius, give us Regulus. These are the mighty ones we understand, and from whom, in a direct line of tradition, we understand Harry of Agincourt, Philip Sidney and our Nelson."

Now since, of the Mediterranean peoples, the Hebrews discovered the Unseen God whom the body of Western civilisation has learnt to worship; since the Greeks invented art, philosophy, letters; since Rome found and developed the idea of imperial government, of imperial colonies as superseding merely fissiparous ones, of settling where she conquered (*ubi Romanus vicit ibi habitat*) and so extending with Government that system of law which Europe still obeys; we cannot be surprised that Israel, Greece, Rome—each in turn—set store on a pure ancestry. Though Christ be the veritable Son of God, his ancestry must be traced back through his supposed father Joseph to the stem of Jesse, and so to Abraham, father of the race. Again, as jealously as the Evangelist claimed

Jesus for a Hebrew of the Hebrews, so, if you will turn to the *Menexenus* of Plato in the Oration of Aspasia over the dead who perished in battle, you hear her claim that "No Pelopes nor Cadmians, nor Egyptians, nor Dauni, nor the rest of the crowd of born foreigners dwell with us; but ours is the land of pure Hellenes, free from admixture." These proud Athenians, as you know, wore brooches in the shape of golden grasshoppers, to signify that they were αὐτόχθονες, children of Attica, sprung direct from her soil. And so, again, the true Roman, while enlarging Rome's citizenship over Asia, Africa, Gaul, to our remote Britain, insisted, even in days of the later Empire, on his pure descent from Æneas and Romulus—

Unde Ramnes et Quirites proque prole posterum
Romuli matrem crearet et nepotem Cæsarem.

With the Ramnes, Quirites, together ancestrally proud as they drew
From Romulus down to our Cæsar—last, best of that blood, of that thew.

Here is a boast that we English must be content to forgo. We may wear a rose on St. George's day, if we are clever enough to grow one. The Welsh, I dare say, have less difficulty with the leek. But April the 23rd is not a time of roses that we can pluck them as we pass, nor can we claim St. George as a compatriot—*Cappadocius nostras.* We have, to be sure, a few legendary heroes, of whom King Arthur and Robin Hood are (I suppose) the greatest; but, save in some Celtic corners of the land, we have few fairies, and these no great matter; while, as for tutelary gods, our springs, our wells, our groves, cliffs, mountain-sides, either never possessed them or possess them no longer. Not of our landscape did it happen that

> The lonely mountains o'er,
> And the resounding shore,
> A voice of weeping heard, and loud lament;
> From haunted spring, and dale
> Edg'd with poplar pale,
> The parting Genius is with sighing sent.

—for the sufficient reason that no tutelary gods of importance were ever here to be dispersed.

Let me press this home upon you by an illustration which I choose with the double purpose of enforcing my argument and sending you to make acquaintance (if you have not already made it) with one of the loveliest poems written in our time.

In one of Pliny's letters you will find a very pleasant description of the source of the Clitumnus, a small Umbrian river which, springing from a rock in a grove of cypresses, descends into the Tinia, a tributary of the Tiber. "Have you ever," writes Pliny to his friend Romanus—

Have you ever seen the source of the Clitumnus? I suppose not, as I never heard you mention it. Let me advise you to go there at once. I have just visited it and am sorry that I put off my visit so long. At the foot of a little hill, covered with old and shady cypress trees, a spring gushes and bursts into a number of streamlets of various size. Breaking, so to speak, forth from its imprisonment, it expands into a broad basin, so clear and transparent that you may count the pebbles and little pieces of money which are thrown into it. From this point the force and weight of the water, rather than the slope of the ground, hurry it onward. What was a mere spring becomes a noble river, broad enough to allow vessels to pass each other as they sail with or against the stream. The current is so strong, though the ground is level, that barges of beam, as they go down, require no assistance of oars; while to go up is as much as can be done with oars and long poles. . . . The banks are clothed with abundant ash and poplar, so distinctly reflected in the transparent waters that they seem to be growing at the bottom of the river and can be counted with ease. The water is as cold as snow and as pure in colour. Hard by the spring stands an ancient and venerable temple with a statue of the river-god Clitumnus, clothed in the customary robe of state. The Oracles here delivered attest the presence of the deity. Close in the precinct stand several little chapels dedicated to particular gods, each of whom owns his distinctive name and special worship, and is the tutelary deity of a runlet. For beside the principal spring, which is, as it were, the parent of all the rest, there are several smaller ones which have their distinct sources but unite their waters with the Clitumnus, over which a bridge is thrown, separating the sacred part of the river from that which is open to general use. Above the bridge you may only go in a boat; below it, you may swim. The people of the town of Hispallum, to whom Augustus gave this place, furnish baths and lodgings at the public expense. There are several small dwelling-houses on the banks, in specially picturesque situations, and they stand quite close to the waterside. In short, everything in the neighbourhood will give you pleasure. You may also amuse yourself with numberless inscriptions on the pillars and walls, celebrating the praises of the stream and of its tutelary god. Many of these you will admire, and some will make you laugh. But no! You are too well cultivated to laugh at such things. Farewell.

Clitumnus still gushes from its rock among the cypresses, as in Pliny's day. The god has gone from his temple, on the frieze of which you may read this later inscription—"*Deus Angelorum, qui fecit Resurrectionem.*" After many centuries and almost in our day, by the brain of Cavour and the sword of Garibaldi, he has made a resurrection for Italy. As part of that resurrection (for no nation can live and be great without its poet) was born a true poet, Carducci. He visited the bountiful, everlasting source, and of what did he sing? Possess yourselves, as for a shilling you may, of his Ode *Alle fonte del Clitumno*, and read: for few nobler poems have adorned our time. He sang of the weeping willow, the ilex, ivy, cypress and the presence of the god still immanent among them. He sang of Umbria, of the ensigns of Rome, of Hannibal swooping down over the Alps; he sang of the nuptials of Janus and Comesena, progenitors of the Italian people; of nymphs, naiads, and the moonlight dances of Oreads; of flocks descending to the river at dusk, of the homestead, the barefooted mother, the clinging child, the father, clad in goat-skins, guiding the ox-waggon; and he ends on the very note of Virgil's famous apostrophe

Sed neque Medorum silvae, ditissima terra . . .

with an invocation of Italy—Italy, mother of bullocks for agriculture, of wild colts for battle, mother of corn and of the vine, Roman mother of enduring laws and mediæval mother of illustrious arts. The mountains, woods and waters of green Umbria applaud the song, and across their applause is heard the whistle of the railway train bearing promise of new industries and a new national life.

E tu, pia madre di giovenchi invitti
a franger glebe e rintegrar maggesi
e d' annitrenti in guerra aspri polledri,
Italia madre,

madre di biade e viti e leggi eterne
ed incliti arti a raddolcir la vita
salve! a te i canti de l' antica lode
io rinovello.

Plaudono i monti al carme e i boschi e l' acque
de l' Umbria verde: in faccia a noi fumando
ed anelando nuove industrie in corsa
fischia il vapore.

And thou, O pious mother of unvanquished
Bullocks to break glebe, to restore the fallow,
And of fierce colts for neighing in the battle:
Italy, mother,

Mother of corn and vines and of eternal
Laws and illustrious arts the life to sweeten,
Hail, hail, all hail! The song of ancient praises
Renew I to thee!

The mountains, woods and waters of green Umbria
Applaud the song: and here before us fuming
And longing for new industries, a-racing
Whistles the white steam.[1]

I put it to you, Gentlemen, that, worthy as are the glories of England to be sung, this note of Carduc-

[1] I quote from a translation by Mr. E. J. Watson, recently published by Messrs. J. W. Arrowsmith, of Bristol.

ci's we cannot decently or honestly strike. Great lives have been bled away into Tweed and Avon: great spirits have been oared down the Thames to Traitor's Gate and the Tower. Deeds done on the Cam have found their way into history. But I once traced the Avon to its source under Naseby battlefield, and found it issuing from the fragments of a stucco swan. No god mounts guard over the head-water of Thames; and the only Englishman who boldly claims a divine descent is (I understand) an impostor who runs an Agapemone. In short we are a mixed race, and our literature is derivative. Let us confine our pride to those virtues, not few, which are honestly ours. A Roman noble, even to-day, has some excuse for reckoning a god in his ancestry, or at least a wolf among its wet-nurses: but of us English even those who came over with William the Norman have the son of a tanner's daughter for escort. I very well remember that, the other day, writers who vindicated our hereditary House of Lords against a certain Parliament Act commonly did so on the ground that since the Reform Bill of 1832, by inclusion of all that was eminent in politics, war and commerce, the Peerage had been so changed as to know itself no longer for the same thing. That is our practical way.

At all events, the men who made our literature had never a doubt, as they were careless to dissimulate, that they were conquering our tongue to bring it into the great European comity, the civilisation of Greece and Rome. An Elizabethan writer, for example, would begin almost as with a formula by begging to be forgiven that he has sought to render the divine accent of Plato, the sugared music of Ovid, into our uncouth and barbarous tongue. There may have been some mock-modesty in this, but it rested on a base of belief. Much of the glory of English Literature was achieved by men who, with the splendour of the Renaissance in their eyes, supposed themselves to be working all the while upon pale and borrowed shadows.

Let us pass the enthusiasms of days when "bliss was it in that dawn to be alive" and come down to Alexander Pope and the Age of Reason. Pope at one time proposed to write a History of English Poetry, and the draft scheme of that History has been preserved. How does it begin? Why thus:—

ERA I.

1. School of Provence	Chaucer's Visions, *Romaunt of the Rose.* *Piers Plowman.* Tales from Boccace. Gower.
2. School of Chaucer	Lydgate. T. Occleve. Walt. de Mapes (a bad error, that!). Skelton.
3. School of Petrarch	E. of Surrey. Sir Thomas Wyatt. Sir Philip Sidney. G. Gascoyn.
4. School of Dante	Lord Buckhurst's *Induction. Gorboduc.* Original of Good Tragedy. Seneca his model.

—and so on. The scheme after Pope's death came into the hands of Gray, who for a time was fired with the notion of writing the History in collaboration with his friend Mason. Knowing Gray's congenital self-distrust, you will not be surprised that in the end he declined the task and handed it over to Warton. But, says Mant in his Life of Warton, "their design"—that is, Gray's design with Mason—"was to introduce specimens of the Provençal poetry, and of the Scaldic, British, and Saxon, as preliminary to what first deserved to be called English poetry, about the time of Chaucer, from whence their history properly so called was to commence." A letter of Gray's on the whole subject, addressed to Warton, is extant, and you may read it in Dr. Courthope's *History of English Poetry.*

Few in this room are old enough to remember the shock of awed surmise which fell upon young minds presented, in the late 'seventies or early 'eighties of the last century, with Freeman's *Norman Conquest* or Green's *Short History of the English People;* in which as through parting clouds of darkness, we beheld our ancestry, literary as well as political, radiantly legitimised; though not, to be sure, in the England that we knew—but far away in Sleswick, happy Sleswick! "Its pleasant pastures, its black-timbered homesteads, its prim little townships looking down on inlets of purple water, were then but a wild waste of heather and sand, girt along the coast with sunless woodland, broken here and there with meadows which crept down to the marshes and to the sea." But what of that? There—surely there, in Sleswick—had been discovered for us our august mother's marriage lines; and if the most of that bright assurance came out of an old political skit, the *Germania* of Tacitus, who recked at the time?

For along followed Mr. Stopford Brooke with an admirable little Primer published at one shilling, to instruct the meanest of us in our common father's actual name—Beowulf.

> *Beowulf* is an old English Epic. . . . There is not one word about our England in the poem. . . . The whole poem, pagan as it is, is English to the very root. It is sacred to us; our Genesis, the book of our origins.

Now I am not only incompetent to discuss with you the more recondite beauties of *Beowulf* but providentially forbidden the attempt by the conditions laid down for this chair. I gather—and my own perusal of the poem and of much writing about it confirms the belief—that it has been largely over-praised by some critics, who have thus naturally provoked others to underrate it. Such things happen. I note, but without subscribing to it, the opinion of Vigfússon and York Powell, the learned editors of the *Corpus Poeticum Boreale*, that in the *Beowulf* we have "an epic completely metamorphosed in form, blown out with long-winded empty repetitions and comments by a book poet, so that one must be careful not to take it as a type of the old poetry," and I seem to hear as from the grave the very voice of my old friend the younger editor in that unfaltering pronouncement. But on the whole I rather incline to accept the cautious surmise of Professor W. P. Ker that "a reasonable view of the merit of *Beowulf* is not impossible, though rash enthusiasm may have made too much of it; while a correct and sober taste may have too contemptuously refused to attend to Grendel and the Firedrake," and to leave it at that. I speak very cautiously because the manner of the late Professor Freeman, in especial, had a knack of provoking in gentle breasts a resentment which the mind in its frailty too easily converted to a prejudice against his matter: while to men trained to admire Thucydides and Tacitus and acquainted with Lucian's "Way to Write History" (Πῶς δεῖ ἱστορίαν συγγράφειν) his loud insistence that the art was not an art but a science, and moreover recently invented by Bishop Stubbs, was a perpetual irritant.

But to return to *Beowulf*—You have just heard the opinions of scholars whose names you must respect. I, who construe Anglo-Saxon with difficulty, must admit the poem to contain many fine, even noble, passages. Take for example Hrothgar's lament for Æschere:—

Hróðgar maþelode, helm Scyldinga:
"Ne frin þú æfter sǽlum; sorh is geniwod

Denigea leódum; deád is Æschere,
Yrmenláfes yldra bróþor,
Mín rún-wita, ond min ræ̆d-bora;
Eaxl-gestealla, ðonne we on orlege
Hafelan wéredon, þonne hniton feþan,
Eoferas cnysedan: swylc scolde eorl wesan
Æþeling æ̆r-gód, swylc Æschere wæs.[1]"

This is simple, manly, dignified. It avoids the besetting sin of the Anglo-Saxon gleeman—the pretentious trick of calling things "out of their right names" for the sake of literary effect (as if *e.g.* the sea could be improved by being phrased into "the seals' domain"). Its Anglo-Saxon *staccato*, so tiresome in sustained narrative, here happens to suit the broken utterance of mourning. In short, it exhibits the Anglo-Saxon Muse at her best, not at her customary. But set beside it a passage in which Homer tells of a fallen warrior—at haphazard, as it were, a single corpse chosen from the press of battle—

πολλὰ δὲ χερμάδια μεγάλ' ἀσπίδας ἐστυφέλιξαν
μαρναμένων ἀμφ' αὐτόν· ὁ δ' ἐν στροφάλιγγι κονίης
κεῖτο μέγας μεγαλωστί, λελασμένος ἱπποσυνάων.

[1] "Hrothgar spake, helm of the Scyldings: Ask not after good tidings. Sorrow is renewed among the Dane-folk. Dead is Æschere, Yrmenlaf's elder brother, who read me rune and bore me rede; comrade at shoulder when we fended our heads in war and the boar-helms rang. Even so should we each be an atheling passing good, as Æschere was."

Can you—can anyone—compare the two passages and miss to see that they belong to two different kingdoms of poetry? I lay no stress here on "architectonics." I waive that the *Iliad* is a well-knit epic and the story of *Beowulf* a shapeless monstrosity. I ask you but to note the difference of note, of accent, of mere music. And I have quoted you but a passage of the habitual Homer. To assure yourselves that he can rise even from this habitual height to express the extreme of majesty and of human anguish in poetry which betrays no false note, no strain upon the store of emotion man may own with self-respect and exhibit without derogation of dignity, turn to the last book of the *Iliad* and read of Priam raising to his lips the hand that has murdered his son. I say confidently that no one unable to distinguish this, as poetry, from the very best of *Beowulf* is fit to engage upon business as a literary critic.

In *Beowulf* then, as an imported poem, let us allow much barbarian merit. It came of dubious ancestry, and it had no progeny. The pretence that our glorious literature derives its lineage from *Beowulf* is in vulgar phrase "a put up job"; a falsehood grafted upon our text-books by Teutonic and Teutonising professors who can bring less evidence for it than will cover a threepenny-piece. Its run for something like that money, in small educational manuals, has been in its way a triumph of pedagogic *réclame.*

Our rude forefathers—the author of *The Rape of the Lock* and of the *Elegy written in a Country Churchyard*—knew nothing of the Exeter and Vercelli Books, nothing of the Ruthwell Cross. But they were poets, practitioners of our literature in the true line of descent, and they knew certain things which all such artists know by instinct. So, before our historians of thirty-odd years ago started to make Chaucer and Beowulf one, these rude forefathers made them two. "Nor am I confident they erred." Rather I am confident, and hope in succeeding lectures to convince you, that, venerable as Anglo-Saxon is, and worthy to be studied as the mother of our vernacular speech (as for a dozen other reasons which my friend Professor Chadwick will give you), its value is historical rather than literary, since from it our Literature is not descended. Let me repeat it in words that admit of no misunderstanding—*From Anglo-Saxon Prose, from Anglo-Saxon Poetry our living Prose and Poetry have, save linguistically, no derivation.* I shall attempt to demonstrate that, whether or not Anglo-Saxon literature, such as it was, died of inherent weakness, die it did, and of its collapse the *Vision of Piers Plowman* may be regarded as the last dying spasm. I shall attempt to convince you that Chaucer did not inherit any secret from Cædmon or Cynewulf, but deserves his old title, "Father of English Poetry," because through Dante, through Boccaccio, through the lays and songs of Provence, he explored back to the Mediterranean, and opened for Englishmen a commerce in the true intellectual mart of Europe. I shall attempt to heap proof on you that whatever the agency—whether through Wyat or Spenser, Marlowe or Shakespeare, or Donne, or Milton, or Dryden, or Pope, or Johnson, or even Wordsworth—always our literature has obeyed, however unconsciously, the precept *Antiquam exquirite matrem*, "Seek back to the ancient mother"; always it has recreated itself, has kept itself pure and strong, by harking back to bathe in those native—yes, *native*—Mediterranean springs.

Do not presume me to be right in this. Rather, if you will, presume me to be wrong until the evidence is laid out for your judgment. But at least understand to-day how profoundly a man, holding that view, must deplore the whole course of academical literary study during these thirty years or so, and how distrust what he holds to be its basal fallacies.

For, literature being written in language, yet being something quite distinct, and the development of our language having been fairly continuous, while the literature of our nation exhibits a false start—a break, silence, repentance, then a renewal on right glorious lines—our students of literature have been drilled to follow the specious continuance while ignoring the actual break, and so to commit the one most fatal error in any study; that of mistaking the inessential for the essential.

As I tried to persuade you in my Inaugural Lecture, our first duty to Literature is to study it absolutely, to understand, in Aristotelian phrase, its τὸ τί ἦν εἶναι; what it *is* and what it *means*. If that be our quest, and the height of it be realised, it is nothing to us—or almost nothing—to know of a certain alleged poet of the fifteenth century, that he helped us over a local or temporary disturbance in our vowel-endings. It is everything to have acquired and to possess such a norm of Poetry within us that we know whether or not what he wrote was POETRY.

Do not think this is easy. The study of right literary criticism is much more difficult than the false path usually trodden; so difficult, indeed, that you may easily count the men who have attempted to grasp the great rules and apply them to writing as an art to be practised. But the names include some very great ones—Aristotle, Horace, Quintilian, Corneille, Boileau, Dryden, Johnson, Lessing, Coleridge, Goethe, Sainte-Beuve, Arnold: and the study, though it may not find its pattern in our time, is not unworthy to be proposed for another attempt before a great University.

IX

On the Lineage of English Literature (II)

SOME of you whose avocations call you, from time to time, to Newmarket may have noted, at a little distance out from Cambridge, a by-road advertised as leading to Quy and Swaffham. It also leads to the site of an old Roman villa: but you need not interrupt your business to visit this, since the best thing discovered there—a piece of tessellated pavement—has been removed and deposited in the Geological Museum in Downing Street, where you may study it very conveniently. It is not at all a first-class specimen of its kind: not to be compared, for example, with the wonderful pavement at Dorchester, or with that (measuring 35 feet by 20) of the great villa unearthed, a hundred years ago, at Stonesfield in Oxfordshire: but I take it as the handiest, and am going to build a small conjecture upon it, or rather a small suggestion of a guess. Remember there is no harm in guessing so long as we do not pretend our guess-work to be something else.

I will ask you to consider first that in these pavements, laid bare for us as "the whistling rustic tends his plough," we have work dating somewhere between the first and fifth centuries, work of unchallengeable beauty, work of a beauty certainly not rivalled until we come to the Norman builders of five or six hundred years later. I want you to let your minds dwell on these long stretches of time—four hundred years or so of Roman occupation (counting, not from Cæsar's raids, but from the serious invasion of 43 A.D. under Aulus Plautius, say to some while after the famous letter of Honorius, calling home the legions). You may safely put it at four hundred years, and then count six hundred as the space before the Normans arrive—a thousand years altogether, or but a fraction—one short generation—less than the interval of time that separates us from King Alfred. In the great Cathedral of Winchester (where sleep, by the way, two gentle writers specially beloved, Isaak Walton and Jane Austen) above the choir-screen to the south, you may see a line of painted chests, of which the inscription on one tells you that it holds what was mortal of King Canute.

> Here are sands, ignoble things,
> Dropp'd from the ruin'd sides of Kings.

But if you walk around to the north of the altar you will find yourself treading on tiles not so very far short of twice that antiquity. Gentlemen, do not think that I would ever speak lightly of our lineage: only let us make as certain as we may what that lineage is.

I want you to-day to understand just what such a pavement as that preserved for your inspection in Downing Street meant to the man who saw it laid and owned it these fifteen hundred years—more or less—ago. *Ubi Romanus vicit, ibi habitat*—"where the Roman has conquered, there he settles": but whether he conquered or settled he carried these small tiles, these *tessellæ*, as religiously as ever Rachel stole her teraphin. "Wherever his feet went there went the tessellated pavement for them to stand on. Even generals on foreign service carried in panniers on muleback the little coloured cubes or *tessellæ* for laying down a pavement in each camping-place, to be taken up again when they moved forward. In England the same sweet emblems of the younger gods of poetic legend, of love, youth, plenty, and all their happy naturalism, are found constantly repeated."[1] I am quoting these sentences from a local historian, but

[1] From *A History of Oxfordshire*, by Mr. J. Meade Falkner, author of Murray's excellent Handbook of Oxfordshire.

you see how these relics have a knack of inspiring prose at once scholarly and imaginative, as (for a more famous instance) the urns disinterred at Walsingham once inspired Sir Thomas Browne's. To continue and adapt the quotation—

> Bacchus with his wild rout, Orpheus playing to a spell-bound audience, Apollo singing to the lyre, Venus in Mars' embrace, Neptune with a host of seamen, scollops, and trumpets, Narcissus by the fountain, Jove and Ganymede, Leda and the swan, wood-nymphs and naiads, satyrs and fauns, masks, hautboys, cornucopiæ, flowers and baskets of golden fruit—what touches of home they must have seemed to these old dwellers in the Cambridgeshire wilds!

Yes, touches of home! For the owner of this villa (you may conceive) is the grandson or even great-great-grandson of the colonist who first built it, following in the wake of the legionaries. The family has prospered and our man is now a considerable landowner. He was born in Britain: his children have been born here: and here he lives a comfortable, well-to-do, out-of-door life, in its essentials I daresay not so very unlike the life of an English country squire to-day. Instead of chasing foxes or hares he hunts the wolf and the wild boar; but the sport is good and he returns with an appetite. He has added a summer parlour to the house, with a northern aspect and no heating-flues; for the old parlour he has enlarged the præfurnium, and through the long winter evenings sits far better warmed than many a master of a modern country-house. A belt of trees on the brow of the rise protects him from the worst winds, and to the south his daughters have planted violet-beds which will breathe odorously in the spring. He has rebuilt and enlarged the slave-quarters and outhouses, replaced the stucco pillars around the atrium with a colonnade of polished stone, and, where stucco remains, has repainted it in fresh colours. He knows that there are no gaps or weak spots in his stockade fence—wood is always cheap. In a word he has improved the estate; is modestly proud of it; and will be content, like the old Athenian, to leave his patrimony not worse but something better than he found it.

Sensible men—and the Romans were eminently that—as a rule contrive to live decently, or, at least, tolerably. What struck Arthur Young more than anything else in his travels through France on the very eve of the Revolution seems to have been the general good-tempered happiness of the French gentry on their estates. We may moralise of the Roman colonists as of the French proprietors that "unconscious of their doom the little victims played"; but we have no right to throw back on them the shadow of what was to come or to cloud the picture of a useful, peaceable, maybe more than moderately happy life, with our later knowledge of disaster mercifully hidden from it.

Although our colonist and his family have all been born in Britain, are happy enough here on the whole, and talk without more than half meaning it, and to amuse themselves with speculations half-wistful, of daring the tremendous journey and setting eyes on Rome some day, their pride is to belong to her, to Rome, the imperial City, the city afar: their windows open back towards her as Daniel's did towards Jerusalem—*Urbs quam dicunt Romam—the* City. Along the great road, hard by, her imperial writ runs. They have never subscribed to the vow of Ruth. "Thy people shall be my people and thy God my God." They dwell under the Pax Romana, not merely protected by it but as *citizens*. Theirs are the ancestral deities portrayed on that unfading pavement in the very centre of the villa—Apollo and Daphne, Bacchus and Ariadne—

> For ever warm and still to be enjoyed,
> For ever panting, and for ever young.

Parcels come to them, forwarded from the near

military station; come by those trade-routes, mysterious to us, concerning which a most illuminating book waits to be written by somebody. There are parcels of seeds—useful vegetables and pot-herbs, helichryse (marigolds as we call them now) for the flower garden, for the colonnade even roses with real Italian earth damp about their roots. There are parcels of books, too—rolls rather, or tablets—wherein the family reads about Rome; of its wealth, the uproar of its traffic, the innumerable chimneys smoking, *fumum et opes strepitumque*. For they are always reading of Rome; feeling themselves, as they read, to belong to it, to be neither savage nor even rustic, but by birthright *of the city*, urbane; and what these exiles read is of how Horace met a bore on the Sacred Road (which would correspond, more or less, with our Piccadilly)—

Along the Sacred Road I strolled one day
Deep in some bagatelle (you know my way)
When up comes one whose face I scarcely knew—
"The dearest of dear fellows! how d'ye do?"
—He grasped my hand. "Well, thanks! The same to you?"

—or of how Horace apologises for protracting a summer jaunt to his country seat:—

Five days I told you at my farm I'd stay,
And lo! the whole of August I'm away.
Well but, Maecenas, you would have me live,
And, were I sick, my absence you'd forgive.
So let me crave indulgence for the fear
Of falling ill at this bad time of year.
When, thanks to early figs and sultry heat,
The undertaker figures with his suite;
When fathers all and fond mammas grow pale
At what may happen to their young heirs male,
And courts and levees, town-bred mortals' ills,
Bring fevers on, and break the seals of wills.[1]

Consider those lines; then consider how long it took the inhabitants of this island—the cultured ones who count as readers or writers—to recapture just that note of urbanity. Other things our forefathers—Britons, Saxons, Normans, Dutch or French refugees—discovered by the way; worthier things if you will; but not until the eighteenth century do you find just that note recaptured; the note of easy confidence that our London had become what Rome had been, the Capital city. You begin to meet it in Dryden; with Addison it is fairly established. Pass a few years, and with Samuel Johnson it is taken for granted. His *London* is Juvenal's Rome, and the same satire applies to one as applied to the other. But against the urbane lines written by one Horace some while

[1] Conington's translation.

before Juvenal let us set a passage from another Horace—Horace Walpole, seventeen hundred years later and some little while ahead of Johnson. He, like our Roman colonist, is a settler in a new country, Twickenham; and like Flaccus he loves to escape from town life.

TWICKENHAM, *June 8th, 1747.*

To the Hon. H. S. CONWAY.

You perceive by my date that I am got into a new camp, and have left my tub at Windsor. It is a little plaything-house that I got out of Mrs. Chevenix's shop, and the prettiest bauble you ever saw. It is set in enamelled meadows with filagree hedges:

> A small Euphrates through the place is roll'd,
> And little finches wave their wings of gold.

Two delightful roads, that *you* would call dusty, supply me continually with coaches and chaises: barges as solemn as Barons of the Exchequer move under my window; Richmond Hill and Ham Walks bound my prospect; but, thank God! the Thames is between me and the Duchess of Queensberry. Dowagers as plenty as flounders inhabit all around, and Pope's ghost is just now skimming under my window by the most poetical moonlight. . . . The Chevenixes had tricked it out for themselves; up two pairs of stairs is what they call Mr. Chevenix's library, furnished with three maps, one shelf, a bust of Sir Isaac Newton and a lame telescope without any glasses. Lord John Sackville *predeceased* me here and instituted certain games called *cricketalia*, which have been celebrated this very evening in honour of him in a neighbouring meadow.

You will think I have removed my philosophy from Windsor with my tea-things hither; for I am writing to you in all tranquillity while a Parliament is bursting about my ears. You know it is going to be dissolved. They say the Prince has taken up two hundred thousand pounds, to carry elections which he won't carry—he had much better have saved it to buy the Parliament after it is chosen.

There you have Horatio Walpole, the man-about-town, almost precisely echoing Horatius Flaccus, the man-about-town; and this (if you will bring your minds to it) is just the sort of passage a Roman colonist in Britain would open upon, out of his parcel of new books, and read, *and understand*, some eighteen hundred years ago.

What became of it all?—of that easy colonial life, of the men and women who trod those tesselated pavements? "Wiped out," say the historians, knowing nothing, merely guessing: for you may with small trouble assure yourselves that the fifth and sixth centuries in the story of this island are a blind spot, concerning which one man's guess may be as good as another's. "Wiped out," they will commonly agree; for while, as I warned you in another lecture, the pedantic mind, faced with a difficulty, tends to remove it conveniently into a category to which it does not belong, still more prone is the pedantic mind to remove it out of existence altogether. So "wiped out" is the theory; and upon it a sympathetic imagination can invent what sorrowful pictures it will of departing legions, the last little cloud of dust down the highway, the lovers by the gate watching it, not comprehending; the peaceful homestead in the background, ripe for doom—and what-not.

Or, stay! There is another theory to which the late Professor Freeman inclined (if so sturdy a figure could be said to incline), laying stress on a passage in Gildas, that the Romans in Britain, faced by the Saxon invader, got together their money, and bolted away into Gaul. "The Romans that were in Britain gathered together their gold-hoard, hid part in the ground and carried the rest over to Gaul," writes Gildas. "The hiding in the ground," says Freeman, "is of course a guess to explain the frequent finding of Roman coins"—which indeed it *does* explain better than the guess that they were carried away, and perhaps better than the schoolboy's suggestion that during their occupation of Britain the Romans spent most of their time in dropping money about. Likely enough, large numbers of the colonists did gather up what they could and flee before the approaching storm; but by no means all, I think. For (since, where all is uncertain, we must reason from what is probable of human nature) in the first place men with large estates do not behave in that way before a danger which creeps upon them little by little, as this Saxon danger did. These colonists could not dig up their fields and carry *them* over to Gaul. They did not keep banking accounts; and in the course of four hundred years their main wealth had certainly been sunk in the land. They could not carry away their villas. We know that many of them did not carry away the *tessellæ* for which (as we have seen) they had so peculiar a veneration; for these remain. Secondly, if the colonists left Britain in a mass, when in the middle of the sixth century we find Belisarius offering the Goths to trade Britain for Sicily, as being "much larger and this long time subservient to Roman rule,"[1] we must suppose either (as Freeman appears to suppose) that Belisarius did not know what he was offering, or that he was attempting a gigantic "bluff," or lastly that he really was offering an exchange not flatly derisory; of which three possible suppositions I prefer the last as the likeliest. Nor am I the less inclined

[1] *Bell. Goth.*, ii., 6.

to choose it, because these very English historians go on to clear the ground in a like convenient way of the Celtic inhabitants, exterminating them as they exterminated the Romans, with a wave of the hand, quite in the fashion of Mr. Podsnap. "This is un-English: therefore for me it merely ceases to exist."

"*Probable extirpation of the Celtic inhabitants,*" jots down Freeman in his margin, and proceeds to write:

> In short, though the literal extirpation of a nation is an impossibility, there is every reason to believe that the Celtic inhabitants of those parts of Britain which had become English at the end of the sixth century had been as nearly extinguished as a nation could be. The women doubtless would be largely spared, but as far as the male sex is concerned we may feel sure that death, emigration, or personal slavery were the only alternatives which the vanquished found at the hands of our fathers.

Upon this passage, if brought to me in an undergraduate essay, I should have much to say. The style, with its abstract nouns ("the literal extirpation of a nation is an impossibility"), its padding and periphrasis ("there is every reason to believe" . . ."as far as the male sex is concerned we may feel sure") betrays the loose thought. It begins with "in short" and proceeds to be long-winded.

It commits what even schoolboys know to be a solecism by inviting us to consider three "alternatives"; and what can I say of "the women doubtless would be largely spared," save that besides scanning in iambics it says what Freeman never meant and what no-one outside of an Aristophanic comedy could ever suggest? "The women doubtless would be largely spared!" It reminds me of the young lady in Cornwall who, asked by her vicar if she had been confirmed, admitted blushingly that "she had reason to believe, partially so."

"The women doubtless would be largely spared!"—But I thank the Professor for teaching me that phrase, because it tries to convey just what I am driving at. The Jutes, Angles, Saxons, did not extirpate the Britons, whatever you may hold concerning the Romans. For, once again, men do not behave in that way, and certainly will not when a live slave is worth money. Secondly, the very horror with which men spoke, centuries after, of Anderida quite plainly indicates that such a wholesale massacre was exceptional, monstrous. If not exceptional, monstrous, why should this particular slaughter have lingered so ineffaceably in their memories? Finally,—and to be as curt as the question deserves—the Celtic Briton in the island was not exterminated and never came near to being exterminated: but on the contrary, remains equipollent with the Saxon in our blood, and perhaps equipollent with that mysterious race we call Iberian, which came before either and endures in this island to-day, as anyone travelling it with eyes in his head can see. Pict, Dane, Norman, Frisian, Huguenot French—these and others come in. If mixture of blood be a shame, we have purchased at the price of that shame the glory of catholicism; and I know of nothing more false in science or more actively poisonous in politics or in the arts than the assumption that we belong as a race to the Teutonic family.

Dane, Norman, Frisian, French Huguenot—they all come in. And will you refuse a hearing when I claim that the Roman came in too? Bethink you how deeply Rome engraved itself on this island and its features. Bethink you that, as human nature is, no conquering race ever lived or could live—even in garrison—among a tributary one without begetting children on it. Bethink you yet further of Freeman's admission that in the wholesale (and quite hypothetical) general massacre "the women doubtless would be largely spared"; and you advance nearer to my point. I see a people which for four hundred years was permeated by Rome. If you insist on its being a Teutonic people (which I flatly deny) then you have one which *alone of Teutonic peoples* has inherited the Roman gift of consolidating conquest, of colonising in the wake of its armies; of driving the road, bridging the ford, bringing the lawless under its sense of law. I see that this nation of ours concurrently, when it seeks back to what alone can inspire and glorify these activities, seeks back, not to any supposed native North, but south to the Middle Sea of our civilisation and steadily to Italy, which we understand far more easily than France—though France has helped us times and again. Putting these things together, I retort upon the ethnologists—for I come from the West of England, where we suffer incredible things from them—"*Semper ego auditor tantum?*" I hazard that the most important thing in our blood is that purple drop of the imperial murex we derive from Rome.

You must, of course, take this for nothing more than it pretends to be—a conjecture, a suggestion. I will follow it up with two statements of fact, neither doubtful nor disputable.

The first is, that when English poetry awoke, long after the Conquest (or, as I should prefer to put it, after the Crusades) it awoke a new thing; in its vocabulary as much like Anglo-Saxon poetry as ever you will, but in metre, rhythm, lilt—and more, in style, feeling, imaginative play—and yet more again, in knowledge of what it aimed to be, in the essentials, in the qualities that make poetry poetry—as different from Anglo-Saxon poetry as cheese is from chalk, and as much more nutritious. Listen to this—

Bytuene Mershe ant Averil
  When spray biginnith to spring,
The lutel foul hath hire wyl
  On hire lud to synge:
Ich libbe in love-longinge
For semlokest of alle thynge,
He may me blisse bringe,
Icham in hire bandoun.
  An hendy hap ichabbe y-hent,
  Ichot from hevene if is me sent,
  From alle wymmen my love is lent,
    And lyht on Alisoun.

Here you have alliteration in plenty; you even have what some hold to be the pattern of Anglo-Saxon alliterative verse (though in practice disregarded, may be, as often as not), the chosen initial used twice in the first line and once at least in the second:

From alle wymmen my *l*ove is *l*ent,
  And *l*yht on A*l*isoun.

But if a man cannot see a difference infinitely deeper than any similarity between this song of Alison and the old Anglo-Saxon verse—*a difference of nature*—I must despair of his literary sense.

What has happened? Well, in Normandy, too, and in another tongue, men are singing much the same thing in the same way:

> A la fontenelle
> Qui sort seur l'araine,
> Trouvai pastorella
> Qui n'iert pas vilaine . . .
>   Merci, merci, douce Marote,
>   N'oçiez pas vostre ami doux,

and this Norman and the Englishman were singing to a new tune, which was yet an old tune re-set to Europe by the Provence, the Roman Province; by the troubadours—Pons de Capdeuil, Bernard de Ventadour, Bertrand de Born, Pierre Vidal, and the rest, with William of Poitou, William of Poitiers. Read and compare; you will perceive that the note then set persists and has never perished. Take Giraud de Borneil—

> Bel companhos, si dormetz o velhatz
> Non dortmatz plus, qu'el jorn es apropchatz—

and set it beside a lyric of our day, written without a thought of Giraud de Borneil—

Heigh! brother mine, art a-waking or a-sleeping:
Mind'st thou the merry moon a many summers fled?
Mind'st thou the green and the dancing and the
    leaping?
Mind'st thou the haycocks and the moon above them
    creeping? . . .

Or take Bernard de Ventadour's—

Quand erba vertz, e fuelha par
E'l flor brotonon per verjan,
E'l rossinhols autet e clar
Leva sa votz e mov son chan,
Joy ai de luy, e joy ai de la flor,
Joy ai de me, e de me dons maior.

Why, it runs straight off into English verse—

When grass is green and leaves appear
  With flowers in bud the meads among,
And nightingale aloft and clear
  Lifts up his voice and pricks his song,
Joy, joy have I in song and flower,
Joy in myself, and in my lady more.

And that may be doggerel; yet what is it but

It was a lover and his lass,
With a hey and a ho and a hey nonino,
That o'er the green cornfield did pass
  In the spring-time, the only pretty ring-time—

or

When daffodils begin to peer,
  With heigh! the doxy over the dale,
Why then comes in the sweet o' the year;
  For the red blood reigns in the winter's pale.

Nay, flatter the Anglo-Saxon tradition by picking its very best—and I suppose it hard to find better than the much-admired opening of Piers Plowman, in which that tradition shot up like the flame of a dying candle:

Bote in a Mayes Morwnynge—on Malverne hulles
Me bi-fel a ferly—a Feyrie me thouhte;
I was weori of wandringe—and wente me to reste
Under a brod banke—bi a Bourne syde,
And as I lay and leonede—and lokede on the watres,
I slumberde in a slepynge—hit sownede so murie.

This is good, solid stuff, no doubt: but tame, inert, if not actually lifeless. As M. Jusserand says of Anglo-Saxon poetry in general, it is like the river Saône—one doubts which way it flows. How tame in comparison with this, for example!—

In somer, when the shawes be sheyne,
  And leves be large and long,
Hit is full mery in feyre foreste
  To here the foulys song:

To se the dere draw to the dale
  And leve the hilles hee,
And shadow hem in the leves grene
  Under the grene-wode tre.

Hit befel on Whitsontide,
  Erly in a May mornyng,
The Son up feyre can shyne,
  And the briddis mery can syng.

"This is a mery mornyng," said litell John,
"Be Hym that dyed on tre;
A more mery man than I am one
Lyves not in Cristianté.

"Pluk up thi hert, my dere mayster,"
Litull John can sey,
"And thynk hit is a full fayre tyme
In a mornyng of May."

There is no doubting which way *that* flows! And this vivacity, this new beat of the heart of poetry, is common to Chaucer and the humblest ballad-maker; it pulses through any book of lyrics printed yesterday, and it came straight to us out of Provence, the Roman Province. It was the Provençal Troubadour who, like the Prince in the fairy tale, broke through the hedge of briers and kissed Beauty awake again.

You will urge that he wakened Poetry not in England alone but all over Europe, in Dante before our Chaucer, in the trouvères and minnesingers as well as in our ballad-writers. To that I might easily retort, "So much the better for Europe, and the more of it the merrier, to win their way into the great comity." But here I put in my second assertion, that we English have had above all nations lying wide of the Mediterranean, the instinct to refresh and renew ourselves at Mediterranean wells; that again and again our writers—our poets especially—have sought them as the hart panteth after the water-brooks. If you accept this assertion, and if you believe as well that our literature, surpassing Rome's, may vie with that of Athens—if you believe that a literature which includes Chaucer, Spenser, Shakespeare, Pope, Wordsworth, Shelley—the Authorised Version of Holy Writ, with Browne, Bunyan, Swift, Addison, Johnson, Arnold, Newman—has entered the circle to take its seat with the first—why then, heartily believing this with you, I leave you to find some better explanation than mine if you can.

But what I content myself with asserting here you can scarcely deny. Chaucer's initial and enormous debt to Dante and Boccaccio stands in as little dispute as Dunbar's to Chaucer. On that favourite poet of mine, Sir Thomas Wyat, I descanted in a former lecture. He is one of your glories here, having entered St. John's College at the age of twelve (which must have been precocious even for those days). Anthony Wood asserts that after finishing his course here, he proceeded to Cardinal Wolsey's new College at Oxford; but, as Christchurch was not founded until 1524, and Wyat, still precocious, had married a wife two years before that, the statement (to quote Dr. Courthope) "seems no better founded than many others advanced by that patriotic but not very scrupulous author." It is more to the point that he went travelling, and brought home from France, Italy, afterwards Spain—always from Latin altars—the flame of lyrical poetry to England; the flame of the Petrarchists, caught from the Troubadours, clarified (so to speak) by the salt of humane letters. On what our Elizabethan literature owes to the Classical revival hundreds of volumes have been written and hundreds more will be written; I will but remind you of what Spenser talked about with Gabriel Harvey, what Daniel disputed with Campion; that Marlowe tried to re-incarnate Machiavelli, that Jonson was a sworn Latinist and the "tribe of Ben" a classical tribe; while, as for Shakespeare, go and reckon the proportion of Italian and Roman names in his *dramatis personæ*. Of Donne's debt to France, Italy, Rome, Greece, you may read much in Professor Grierson's great edition, and I daresay Professor Grierson would be the first to allow that all has not yet been computed. You know how Milton prepared himself to be a poet. Have you realised that, in those somewhat strangely constructed sonnets of his, Milton was deliberately modelling upon the Horatian Ode, as his *confrère*, Andrew Marvell, was avowedly attempting the like in his famous *Horatian Ode* on Cromwell's Return from Ireland; so that if Cromwell had returned (like Mr. Quilp), walked in and caught his pair of Latin Secretaries scribbling verse, one at either end of the office table, both might colourably have pleaded that they were, after all, writing Latin. Waller's task in poetry was to labour true classical polish where Cowley laboured sham-classical form. Put together Dryden's various Prefaces and you will find them one solid monument to his classical faith. Of Pope, Gray, Collins, you will not ask me to speak. What is salt in Cowper you can taste only when you have detected that by a stroke of madness he missed, or barely missed, being our true English Horace, that almost more nearly than the rest he hit what the rest had been seeking. Then, of the "romantic revival"—enemy of false classicism, not of classicism—bethink you what, in his few great years, Wordsworth owed directly to France of the early Revolution; what Keats drew forth out of Lemprière: and again bethink you how Tennyson wrought upon Theocritus, Virgil, Catullus; upon what Arnold constantly shaped his verse; how Browning returned ever upon Italy to inspire his best and correct his worse.

Of Anglo-Saxon prose I know little indeed, but enough of the world to feel reasonably sure that if it contained any single masterpiece—or anything that could be paraded as a masterpiece—we should have heard enough about it long before now. It was invented by King Alfred for excellent political reasons; but, like other ready-made political inventions in this country, it refused to thrive. I think it can be demonstrated, that the true line of intellectual descent in prose lies through Bede (who wrote in Latin, the "universal language"), and not through the Blickling Homilies, or Ælfric, or the Saxon Chronicle. And I am sure that Freeman is perversely wrong when he laments as a "great mistake" that the first Christian missionaries from Rome did not teach their converts to pray and give praise in the vernacular. The vernacular being what it was, these men did better to teach the religion of the civilised world—*orbis terrarum*—in the language of the civilised world. I am not thinking of its efficiency for spreading the faith; but neither is Freeman; and, for that, we must allow these old missionaries to have known their own business. I am thinking only of how this "great mistake" affected our literature; and if you will read Professor Saintsbury's *History of English Prose Rhythm* (pioneer work which yet wonderfully succeeds in illustrating what our prose-writers from time to time were trying to do); if you will study the Psalms in the Authorised Version; if you will consider what Milton, Clarendon, Sir Thomas Browne, were aiming at; what Addison, Gibbon, Johnson; what Landor, Thackeray, Newman, Arnold, Pater; I doubt not your rising from the perusal convinced that our nation, in this storehouse of Latin to refresh and replenish its most sacred thoughts, has enjoyed a continuous blessing: that the Latin of the Vulgate and the Offices has been a background giving depth and, as the painters say, "value" to nine-tenths of our serious writing.

And now, since this and the previous lecture run something counter to a great deal of that teaching in English Literature which nowadays passes most acceptably, let me avoid offence, so far as may be, by defining one or two things I am *not* trying to do.

I am not persuading you to despise your linguistic descent. English is English—our language; and all its history to be venerated by us.

I am not persuading you to despise linguistic study. *All* learning is venerable.

I am not persuading you to behave like Ascham, and turn English prose into pedantic Latin; nor would I have you doubt that in the set quarrel between Campion, who wished to divert English verse into strict classical channels, and Daniel, who vindicated our free English way (derived from Latin through the Provençal), Daniel was on the whole, right, Campion on the whole, wrong: though I believe that both ways yet lie open, and we may learn, if we study them intelligently, a hundred things from the old classical metres.

I do not ask you to forget what there is of the Northmen in your blood. If I desired this, I could not worship William Morris as I do, among the later poets.

I do not ask you to doubt that the barbarian invaders from the north, with their myths and legends, brought new and most necessary blood of imagination into the literary material—for the time almost exhausted—of Greece and Rome.

Nevertheless, I do contend that when Britain (or, if you prefer it, Sleswick)

> When Sleswick first at Heaven's command
> Arose from out the azure main,

she differed from Aphrodite, that other foam-born, in sundry important features of ear, of lip, of eye.

Lastly, if vehement assertions on the one side have driven me into too vehement dissent on the other, I crave pardon; not for the dissent but for the vehemence, as sinning against the very principle I would hold up to your admiration—the old Greek principle of avoiding excess.

But I *do* commend the patient study of Greek and Latin authors—in the original or in translation—to all of you who would write English; and for three reasons.

(1) In the first place they will correct your insularity of mind; or, rather, will teach you to forget it. The Anglo-Saxon, it has been noted, ever left an empty space around his houses; and that, no doubt, is good for a house. It is not so good for the mind.

(2) Secondly, we have a tribal habit, confirmed by Protestant meditation upon a Hebraic religion, of confining our literary enjoyment to the written word and frowning down the drama, the song, the dance. A fairly attentive study of modern lyrical verse has persuaded me that this exclusiveness may be carried too far, and threatens to be deadening. "I will sing and give praise," says the Scripture, "with the best member that I have"—meaning the tongue. But the old Greek was an "all-round man" as we say. He sought to praise and give thanks with all his members,

and to tune each to perfection. I think his way worth your considering.

(3) Lastly, and chiefly, I commend these classical authors to you because they, in the European civilisation which we all inherit, conserve the norm of literature; the steady grip on the essential; the clean outline at which in verse or in prose—in epic, drama, history, or philosophical treatise—a writer should aim.

So sure am I of this, and of its importance to those who think of writing, that were this University to limit me to three texts on which to preach English Literature to you, I should choose the Bible in our Authorised Version, Shakespeare, and Homer (though it were but in a prose translation). Two of these lie outside my marked province. Only one of them finds a place in your English school. But Homer, who comes neither within my map, nor within the ambit of the Tripos, would—because he most evidently holds the norm, the essence, the secret of all—rank first of the three for my purpose.

X

English Literature in our Universities (I)

ALL lectures are too long. Towards the close of my last, Gentlemen, I let fall a sentence which, heard by you in a moment of exhausted or languid interest, has since, like enough, escaped your memory even if it earned passing attention. So let me repeat it, for a fresh start.

Having quoted to you the words of our Holy Writ, "I will sing and give praise with the best member that I have," I added, "But the old Greek was an 'all-round' man; he sought to praise and give thanks with all his members, and to tune each to perfection." Now a great many instructive lectures might be written on that text: nevertheless you may think it a strange one, and obscure, for the discourse on "English Literature in our Universities" which, according to promise, I must now attempt.

The term "an all-round man" may easily mislead you unless you take it with the rest of the sentence and particularly with the words "praise and give thanks." Praise *whom?* Give thanks to *whom?* To *whom* did our Greek train all his members to render adoration?

Why, to the gods—his gods: to Zeus, Apollo, Aphrodite; and from them down to the lesser guardian deities of the hearth, the field, the farmstead. We modern men suffer a double temptation to misunderstand, by belittling, the reverence in which Hellas and Rome held their gods. To start with, our religion has superseded theirs. We approach the Olympians with no bent towards venerating them; with minds easy, detached, to which a great deal of their theology—the amativeness of Zeus for example—must needs seem broadly comic, and a great deal of it not only comic but childish. We are encouraged in this, moreover, when we read such writers as Aristophanes and Lucian, and observe how they poked fun at the gods. We assume—so modern he seems—Aristophanes' attitude towards his immortals to be ours; that when, for example, Prometheus walks on to the stage under an umbrella, to hide himself from the gaze of all-seeing Zeus, the Athenian audience laughed just as we laugh who have read Voltaire. Believe me, they laughed quite differently; believe me, Aristophanes and Voltaire had remarkably different minds and worked on utterly different backgrounds. Believe me, you will understand Aristophanes only less than you will understand Æschylus himself if you confuse Aristophanes' mockery of Olympus with modern mockery. But, if you will not take my word for it, let me quote what Professor Gilbert Murray said, the other day, speaking before the English Association on Greek poetry, how constantly connected it is with religion:

> "All thoughts, all passions, all desires". . .In our Art it is true, no doubt, that they are "the ministers of love"; in Greek they are as a whole the ministers of religion, and this is what in a curious degree makes Greek poetry matter, makes it relevant. There is a sense in each song of a relation to the whole of things, and it was apt to be expressed with the whole body, or, one may say, the whole being.[1]

To a Greek, in short, his gods mattered enormously; and to a Roman. To a Roman they continued to matter enormously, down to the end. Do you remember that tessellated pavement with its emblems and images of the younger gods? and how I told you that a Roman general on foreign service would carry the little cubes in panniers

[1] *What English Poetry may still learn from Greek:* a paper read before the English Association on Nov. 17, 1911.

on mule-back, to be laid down for his feet at the next camping-place? Will you suggest that he did this because they were pretty? You know that practical men—conquering generals—don't behave in that way. He did it because they were sacred; because, like most practical men, he was religious, and his gods must go with him. They filled his literature: for why? He believed himself to be sprung from their loins. Where would Latin literature be, for example, if you could cut Venus out of it? Consider Lucretius' grand invocation:

> Æneadum genetrix, hominum divumque voluptas,
> Alma Venus!

Consider the part Virgil makes her play as moving spirit of his whole great poem. So follow her down to the days of the later Empire and open the *Pervigilium Veneris* and discover her, under the name of Dione, still the eternal Aphrodite sprung from the foam amid the churning hooves of the sea-horses—*inter et bipedes equos:*—

> Time was that a rain-cloud begat her, impregning the heave of the deep,
> 'Twixt hooves of sea-horses a-scatter, stampeding the dolphins as sheep.
> Lo! arose of that bridal Dione, rainbow'd and besprent of its dew!
> *Now learn ye to love who loved never—now ye who have loved, love anew!*

Her favour it was fill'd the sails of the Trojan for
Latium bound,
Her favour that won her Æneas a bride on Laurentian
ground,
And anon from the cloister inveigled the Virgin, the
Vestal, to Mars;
As her wit by the wild Sabine rape recreated her Rome
for its wars
With the Ramnes, Quirites, together ancestrally proud
as they drew
From Romulus down to our Cæsar—last, best of that
blood, of that thew.
*Now learn ye to love who loved never—now ye who have
loved, love anew!*

"Last, best of that blood"—her blood, *fusa Paphies de cruore*, and the blood of Teucer, *revocato a sanguine Teucri*, "of that thew"—the thew of Tros and of Mars. Of these and no less than these our Roman believed himself the son and inheritor.

If we grasp this, that the old literature was packed with the old religion, and not only packed with it but permeated by it, we have within our ten fingers the secret of the "Dark Ages," the real reason why the Christian Fathers fought down literature and almost prevailed to the point of stamping it out. They hated it, not as literature; or at any rate, not to begin with; nor, to begin with, because it happened to be voluptuous and they austere: but they hated it because it held in its very texture, not to be separated, a religion over which they had hardly triumphed, a religion actively inimical to that of Christ, inimical to truth; so that for the sake of truth and in the name of Christ they had to fight it, accepting no compromise, yielding no quarter, foreseeing no issue save that one of the twain—Jupiter or Christ, Deus Optimus Maximus or the carpenter's son of Nazareth—must go under.

It all ended in compromise, to be sure; as all struggles must between adversaries so tremendous. To-day, in Dr. Smith's *Classical Dictionary*, Origen rubs shoulders with Orpheus and Orcus; Tertullian reposes cheek by jowl with Terpsichore. But we are not concerned, here, with what happened in the end. We are concerned with what these forthright Christian fighters had in their minds—to trample out the old literature *because* of the false religion. Milton understood this, and was thinking of it when he wrote of the effect of Christ's Nativity—

> The Oracles are dumb;
> No voice or hideous hum
> Runs through the archèd roof in words deceiving.
> Apollo from his shrine
> Can no more divine,
> With hollow shriek the steep of Delphos leaving.
> No nightly trance, or breathèd spell

Inspires the pale-eyed Priest from the prophetic cell.

The lonely mountains o'er,
And the resounding shore,
A voice of weeping heard, and loud lament;
From haunted spring, and dale
Edg'd with poplar pale,
The parting Genius is with sighing sent;
With flower-inwoven tresses torn
The Nymphs in twilight shade of tangled thickets mourn.

—as Swinburne understands and expresses it in his *Hymn to Proserpine*, supposed to be chanted by a Roman of the "old profession" on the morrow of Constantine's proclaiming the Christian faith:—

O Gods dethroned and deceased, cast forth, wiped out in a day!
From your wrath is the world released, redeem'd from your chains, men say.
New Gods are crown'd in the city; their flowers have broken your rods;
They are merciful, clothed with pity, the young compassionate Gods.
But for me their new device is barren, the days are bare;
Things long past over suffice, and men forgotten that were. . .
Wilt thou yet take all, Galilean? but these thou shalt not take,
The laurel, the palms and the paean, the breasts of the nymphs in the brake;

Thou hast conquer'd, O pale Galilean; the world has
grown grey from thy breath;
We have drunken of things Lethean, and fed on the
fullness of death.

"Thou hast conquer'd, O pale Galilean!" However the struggle might sway in this or that other part of the field, Literature had to be beaten to her knees, and still beaten flat until the breath left her body. You will not be surprised that the heavy hand of these Christian Fathers fell first upon the Theatre: for the actor in Rome was by legal definition an "infamous" man, even as in England until the other day he was by legal definition a vagabond and liable to whipping. The policy of religious reformers has ever been to close the theatres, as our Puritans did in 1642; and a recent pronouncement by the Bishop of Kensington would seem to show that the instinct survives to this day. Queen Elizabeth—like her brother, King Edward VI—signalised the opening of a new reign by inhibiting stage-plays; and I invite you to share with me the pensive speculation, "How much of English Literature, had she not relented, would exist to-day for a King Edward VII Professor to talk about?" Certainly the works of Shakespeare would not; and that seems to me a thought so impressive as to deserve the attention of bishops as well as of kings.

Apart from this instinct the Christian Fathers, it would appear, had plenty of provocation. For the actors, who had jested with the Old Religion on a ground of accepted understanding—much as a good husband (if you will permit the simile) may gently tease his wife, not loving her one whit the less, taught by affection to play without offending—had mocked at the New Religion in a very different way: savagely, as enemies, holding up to ridicule the Church's most sacred mysteries. Tertullian, in an uncompromising treatise *De Spectaculis*, denounces stage-plays root and branch; tells of a demon who entered into a woman in a theatre and on being exorcised pleaded that the mistake might well be excused, since he had found her in his own demesne. Christians should avoid these shows and await the greatest *spectaculum* of all—the Last Judgment. "Then," he promises genially, "will be the time to listen to the tragedians, whose lamentations will be more poignant, for their proper pain. Then will the comedians turn and twist in capers rendered nimbler than ever by the sting of the fire that is not quenched." By 400 A.D. Augustine cries triumphantly that the theatres are falling—the very walls of them tumbling—throughout the Empire. "*Per omnes paene civitates cadunt theatra . . . cadunt et fora vel moenia in quibus demonia colebantur;*" the very walls within which these devilments were practised. But the fury is unabated and goes on stamping down the embers. In the eighth century our own Alcuin (as the school of Freeman would affectionately call him) is no less fierce. All plays are anathema to him, and he even disapproves of dancing bears—though not, it would appear, of bad puns: "*nec tibi sit ursorum saltantium cura, sed clericorum psallentium.*"[1]

The banning of *all* literature you will find harder to understand; nay impossible, I believe, unless you accept the explanation I gave you. Yet there it is, an historical fact. "What hath it profited posterity—*quid posteritas emolumenti tulit,*" wrote Sulpicius Severus, about 400 A.D., "to read of Hector's fighting or Socrates' philosophising?" Pope Gregory the Great—St. Gregory, who sent us the Roman missionaries—made no bones about it at all. "*Quoniam non cognovi literaturam,*" he quoted approvingly from the 70th Psalm, "*introibo in potentias Domini*": "*Because* I know nothing of

[1] See Mr. E. K. Chambers's *Mediaeval Stage*, Dr. Courthope's *History of English Poetry*, and Professor W. P. Ker's *The Dark Ages*.

literature I shall enter into the strength of the Lord." "The praises of Christ cannot be uttered in the same tongue as those of Jove," writes this same Gregory to Desiderius, Archbishop of Vienne, who had been rash enough to introduce some of his young men to the ancient authors, with no worse purpose than to teach them a little grammar. Yet no one was prouder than this Pope of the historical Rome which he had inherited. Alcuin, again, forbade the reading of Virgil in the monastery over which he presided: it would sully his disciples' imagination. "How is this, *Virgilian!*" he cried out upon one taken in the damnable act,—"that without my knowledge and against my order thou hast taken to studying Virgil?" To put a stop to this unhallowed indulgence the clergy solemnly taught that Virgil was a wizard.

To us, long used as we are to the innocent gaieties of the Classical Tripos, these measures to discourage the study of Virgil may appear drastic, as the mental attitude of Gregory and Alcuin towards the Latin hexameter (so closely resembling that of Byron towards the waltz) not far removed from foolishness. But there you have in its quiddity the mediaeval mind: and the point I now put to you is, that *out of this soil our universities grew.*

We, who claim Oxford and Cambridge for our nursing mothers, have of all men least excuse to forget it. A man of Leyden, of Louvain, of Leipzig, of Berlin, may be pardoned that he passes it by. More than a hundred years ago Salamanca had the most of her stones torn down to make defences against Wellington's cannon. Paris, greatest of all, has kept her renown; but you shall search the slums of the Latin Quarter in vain for the sixty or seventy colleges that before the close of the fifteenth century, had arisen to adorn her, the intellectual Queen of Europe. In Bologna, the ancient and stately, almost alone among the continental universities, survive a few relics of the old collegiate system—the College of Spain, harbouring some five or six students, and a little house founded for Flemings in 1650: and in Bologna the system never attained to real importance.

But in England where, great as London is, the national mind has always harked to the country for the graces of life, so that we seem by instinct to see it as only desirable in a green setting, our universities, planted by the same instinct on lawns watered by pastoral streams, have suffered so little and received so much from the years that now we can hardly conceive of Oxford or Cambridge as ruined save by "the unimaginable touch of Time." Of all the secular Colleges bequeathed to Oxford, she has lost not one; while Cambridge (I believe) has parted only with Cavendish. Some have been subsumed into newer foundations; but always the process has been one of merging, of blending, of justifying the new bottle by the old wine. The vengeance of civil war—always very much of a family affair in England—has dealt tenderly with Oxford and Cambridge; the more calculating malignity of Royal Commissions not harshly on the whole. University reformers may accuse both Oxford and Cambridge of

> Annihilating all that's made
> To a green thought in a green shade:

but with those sour men we have nothing here to do: like Isaak Walton's milkmaid we will not "load our minds with any fears of many things that will never be."

But, as they stand, Oxford and Cambridge—so amazingly alike while they play at differences, and both so amazingly unlike anything else in the wide world—do by a hundred daily reminders connect us with the Middle Age, or, if you prefer Arnold's phrase, whisper its lost enchantments. The cloister, the grave grace in hall, the chapel bell, the men hurrying into their surplices or to lectures "with the wind in their gowns," the staircase, the nest of chambers within the oak—all these softly reverberate over our life here, as from belfries, the mediaeval mind.

And that mediaeval mind actively hated (of partial acquaintance or by anticipation) almost everything we now study! Between it and us, except these memorials, nothing survives to-day but the dreadful temptation to learn, the dreadful instinct in men, as they grow older and wiser, to trust learning after all and endow it—that, and the confidence of a steady stream of youth.

The Universities, then, sprang out of mediaeval life, out of the mediaeval mind; and the mediaeval mind had for centuries been taught to abominate literature. I would not exaggerate or darken the "Dark Ages" for you by throwing too much bitumen into the picture. I know that at the beginning there had been a school of Origen which advocated the study of Greek poetry and philosophy, as well as the school of Tertullian which condemned it. There is evidence that the "humanities" were cultivated here and there and after a fashion behind Gregory's august back. I grant that, while in Alcuin's cloister (and Alcuin, remember, became a sort of Imperial Director of Studies in Charlemagne's court) the wretched monk who loved Virgil had to study him with an illicit candle, to copy him with numbed fingers in a corner of the bitter-cold cloister, on the other hand many beautiful manuscripts preserved to us bear witness of cloisters where literature was tolerated if not officially honoured. I would not have you so uncritical as to blame the Church or its clergy for what happened; as I would have you remember that if the Church killed literature, she—and, one may say, she alone—kept it alive.

Yet, and after all these reservations, it remains true that Literature had gone down disastrously. Even philosophy, unless you count the pale work of Boethius—*real* philosophy had so nearly perished that men possessed no more of Aristotle than a fragment of his Logic, and "*the* Philosopher" had to creep back into Western Europe through translations from the Arabic! But this is the point I wish to make clear.—Philosophy came back in the great intellectual revival of the twelfth century, Literature did not. Literature's hour had not come. Men had to catch up on a dreadful leeway of ignorance. The form did not matter as yet: they wanted science—to know. I should say, rather, that as yet form *seemed* not to matter: for in fact form always matters: the personal always matters: and you cannot explain the vast crowds Abelard drew to Paris save by the fascination in the man, the fire communicated by the living voice. Moreover (as in a previous lecture I tried to prove) you cannot divorce accurate thought from accurate speech; but for accuracy, even for hair-splitting accuracy, of speech the universities had the definitions of the Schoolmen. In literature they had yet to discover a concern. Literature was a thing of the past, inanimate. Nowhere in Europe could it be felt even to breathe. To borrow a beautiful phrase of Wordsworth's, men numbered it among "things silently gone out of mind or things violently destroyed."

Nobody quite knows how these Universities began. Least of all can anybody tell how Oxford and Cambridge began. In Bede, for instance—that is, in England as the eighth century opens—we see scholarship already moving towards the *thing*, treading with sure instinct towards the light. Though a hundred historians have quoted it, I doubt if a feeling man who loves scholarship can read the famous letter of Cuthbert describing Bede's end and not come nigh to tears.

And Bede's story contains no less wonder than beauty, when you consider how the fame of this holy and humble man of heart, who never left his cloisters at Jarrow, spread over Europe, so that, though it sound incredible, our Northumbria narrowly missed in its day to become the pole-star of Western culture. But he was a disinterested genius, and his pupil, Alcuin, a pushing dull man and a born reactionary; so that, while Alcuin scored the personal success and went off to teach in the court of Charlemagne, the great chance was lost.

No one knows when the great Universities were founded, or precisely out of what schools they grew; and you may derive amusement from the historians when they start to explain how Oxford and Cambridge in particular came to be chosen for sites. My own conjecture, that they were chosen for the extraordinary salubrity of their climates, has met (I regret to say) with derision, and may be set down to the caprice of one who ever inclines to think the weather good where he is happy. Our own learned historian, indeed—Mr. J. Bass Mullinger—devotes some closely reasoned pages to proving that Cambridge was chosen as the unlikeliest spot in the world, and is driven to quote the learned Poggio's opinion that the unhealthiness of a locality recommended it as a place of education for youth; as Plato, knowing naught of Christianity but gifted with a soul naturally Christian, "*had selected a noisome spot for his Academe, in order that the mind might be strengthened by the weakness of the body.*" So difficult still it is for the modern mind to interpret the mediaeval!

Most likely these Universities grew as a tree grows from a seed blown by chance of the wind. It seems easy enough to understand why Paris, that great city, should have possessed a great University; yet I surmise the processes at Oxford and Cambridge to have been only a little less fortuitous. The schools of Remigius and of William of Champeaux (we will say) have given Paris a certain prestige, when Abelard, a pupil of William's, springs into fame and draws a horde of students from all over Europe to sit at his feet. These "nations" of young men have to be organised, brought under some sort of discipline, if only to make the citizens' lives endurable: and lo! the thing is done. In like manner Irnerius at Bologna, Vacarius at Oxford, and at Cambridge some innominate teacher, "of importance," as Browning would put it, "in his day," possibly set the ball rolling; or again it is suggested that a body of scholars dissatisfied with Oxford (such dissatisfaction has been known even in historical times) migrated hither—a laborious journey, even nowadays—and that so

A brighter Hellas rears its mountains
From waves serener far!

These young or nascent bodies had a trick of breaking away after this fashion. For reasons no longer obvious they hankered specially towards Stamford or Northampton. Until quite recently, within living memory, all candidates for a Mastership of Arts at Oxford had to promise never to lecture at Stamford. A flood here in 1520, which swept away Garret Hostel Bridge, put Cambridge in like mind and started a prophecy (to which you may find allusion in the fourth book of *The Faerie Queene*) that both Universities would meet in the end, and kiss, at Stamford. Each in turn broke away from Northampton, and the worthy Fuller (a Northamptonshire man) has recorded his wonder that so eligible a spot was not finally chosen.

I have mentioned a flood: but the immediate cause of these migrations or attempted migrations were not usually respectable enough to rank with any such act of God. They started as a rule with some Town and Gown row, or some bloody affray between scholars of the North and of the South. Without diminishing your sense of the real fervour for learning which drew young men from the remotest parts of Europe to these centres, but having for my immediate object to make clear to you that, whatever these young men sought, it was not literature, I wish you first to have in your minds a vivid picture of what a university town was like, and what its students were like during the greater part of the 12th and 13th centuries; that is to say, after the first enthusiasm had died down, when Oxford or Cambridge had organised itself into a *Studium Generale*, or *Universitas* (which, of course, has nothing to do with Universality, whether of teaching or of frequenting, but simply means a society. *Universitas* = all of us).

To begin with, the town was of wood, often on fire in places; with the alleviation of frequent winter floods, which in return, in the words of a modern poet, would "leave a lot of little things behind them." It requires but a small effort of the imagination in Cambridge to picture the streets as narrow, dark, almost meeting overhead in gables out of which the house slops would be discharged after casual warning down into a central gutter. That these narrow streets were populous with students remains certain, however much discount we allow on contemporary bills of reckoning. And the crowd was noisy. Men have always been ingenious in their ways of celebrating academical success. Pythagoras, for example, sacrificed an ox on solving the theorem numbered 47 in the first book of Euclid; and even to-day a professor in his solitary lodge may be encouraged to believe now and then, from certain evidences in the sky, that the spirit of Pythagoras is not dead but translated.

But of the mediaeval University the lawlessness, though well attested, can scarcely be conceived. When in the streets "nation" drew the knife upon "nation," "town" upon "gown"; when the city bell started to answer the clang of St. Mary's; horrible deeds were done. I pass over massacres, tumults such as the famous one of St. Scholastica's Day at Oxford and choose one at a decent distance (yet entirely typical) exhumed from the annals of the University of Toulouse, in the year 1332. In that year

Five brothers of the noble family de la Penne lived together in a Hospicium at Toulouse as students of the Civil and Canon Law. One of them was Provost of a Monastery, another Archdeacon of Albi, another an Archpriest, another Canon of Toledo. A bastard son of their father, named Peter, lived with them as squire to the Canon. On Easter Day, Peter, with another squire of the household named Aimery Béranger and other students, having dined at a tavern, were dancing with women, singing, shouting, and beating "metallic vessels and iron culinary instruments" in the street before their master's house. The Provost and the Archpriest were sympathetically watching the jovial scene from a window, until it was disturbed by the appearance of a Capitoul and his officers, who summoned some of the party to surrender the prohibited arms which they were wearing. "*Ben Senhor, non fassat*" was the impudent reply. The Capitoul attempted to arrest one of the offenders; whereupon the ecclesiastical party made a combined attack upon the official. Aimery Béranger struck him in the face with a poignard, cutting off his nose and part of his chin and lips, and knocking out or breaking no less than eleven teeth. The surgeons deposed that if he recovered (he eventually did recover) he would never be able to speak intelligibly. One of the watch was killed outright by Peter de la Penne. That night the murderer slept, just as if nothing had happened, in the house of his ecclesiastical masters. The whole household, masters and servants alike, were, however, surprised by the other Capitouls and a crowd of 200 citizens, and led off to prison, and the house is alleged to have been pillaged. The Archbishop's Official demanded their surrender. In the case of the superior ecclesiastics this, after a short delay, was granted. But Aimery, who dressed like a layman in "divided and striped clothes" and wore a long beard, they refused to treat as a clerk, though it was afterwards alleged that the tonsure was plainly discernible upon his head until it was shaved by order of the Capitouls. Aimery was put to the torture, admitted his crime, and was sentenced to death. The sentence was carried out by hanging, after he had had his hand cut off on the scene of the crime, and been dragged by horses to the place of execution. The Capitouls were then excommunicated by the Official, and the ecclesiastical side of the quarrel was eventually transferred to the Roman Court. Before the Parlement of Paris the University complained of the violation of the Royal privilege exempting scholars' servants from the ordinary tribunals. The Capitouls were imprisoned, and after long litigation sentenced to pay enormous damages to the ruffian's family and erect a chapel for the good of his soul. The city was condemned for a time to the forfeiture of all its privileges. The body was cut down from the gibbet on which it had been hanging for three years, and accorded a solemn funeral. Four Capitouls bore the pall, and all fathers of families were required to walk in the procession. When they came to the Schools, the citizens solemnly begged pardon of the University, and the *cortège* was joined by 5000 scholars. Finally, it cost the city 15,000 *livres tournois* or more to regain their civic privileges.[1]

The late Mr. Cecil Rhodes once summarised all Fellows of Colleges as children in matters of finance. Be that as it may, you will find nothing more constant in history than the talent of the universities for extracting money or money's worth out of a riot. Time (I speak as a parent) has scarcely blunted that faculty; and still—since

[1] Rashdall, *The Universities of Europe in the Middle Ages*, vol. ii, p. 684, from documents printed in Fournier's collection.

where young men congregate, noise there must be—our Universities like Wordsworth's Happy Warrior

> turn their necessity to glorious gain.

These were the excesses of young "bloods," and their servants: but with them mingled scholars not less ferocious in their habits because almost desperately poor. You all know, I dare say, that very poor scholars would be granted licences to beg by the Chancellor. The sleeve of this gown in which I address you represents the purse or pocket of a Master of Arts, and may hint to you by its amplitude how many crusts he was prepared to receive from the charitable.

Now, choosing to ignore (because it has been challenged as overpainted) a picture of penury endured by the scholars of St. John's College in this University, let me tell you two stories, one well attested, the other fiction if you will, but both agreeable as testifying to the spirit of youth which, ever blowing upon their sacred embers, has kept Oxford and Cambridge perennially alive.

My first is of three scholars so poor that they possessed but one "cappa" and gown between them. They took it in turns therefore, and when one went to lecture the other two kept to their lodgings. I invite you even to reflect on the joy of the lucky one, in a winter lecture room, dark, with unglazed windows, as he listened and shuffled his feet for warmth in the straw of the floor. [No one, by the way, can understand the incessant harping of our early poets upon May-time and the return of summer until he has pictured to himself the dark and cold discomfort of a Middle-English winter.] These three poor scholars fed habitually on bread, with soup and a little wine, tasting meat only on Sundays and feasts of the Church. Yet one of them, Richard of Chichester, who lived to become a saint, *saepe retulit quod nunquam in vita sua tam jucundam, tam delectabilem duxerat vitam*—that never had he lived so jollily, so delectably.

That is youth, youth blessed by friendship. Now for my second story, which is also of youth and friendship.—

Two poor scholars, who had with pains become Masters of Arts and saved their pence to purchase the coveted garb, on the afternoon of their admission took a country walk in it, together flaunting their new finery. But, the day being gusty, on their return across the bridge, a puff of wind caught the *biretta* of one and blew it into the river. The loss was irrecoverable, since neither could swim.

The poor fellow looked at his friend. His friend looked at him. "Between us two," he said, "it is all or naught," and cast his own cap to float and sink with the other down stream.

You will never begin to understand literature until you understand something of life. These young men, your forerunners, understood something of life while as yet completely careless of literature. After the impulse of Abelard and others had died down, the mass of students betook themselves to the universities, no doubt, for quite ordinary, mercenary reasons. The University led to the Church, and the Church, in England at any rate, was the door to professional life.

Nearly all the civil servants of the Crown—I am here quoting freely—the diplomatists, the secretaries or advisers of great nobles, the physicians, the architects, at one time the secular lawgivers, all through the Middle Ages the then large tribe of ecclesiastical lawyers, were ecclesiastics. . . . Clerkship did not necessarily involve even minor orders. But as it was cheaper to a king or a bishop or a temporal magnate to reward his physician, his legal adviser, his secretary, or his agent by a Canonry or a Rectory than by large salaries, the average student of Paris or Oxford or Cambridge looked toward the Church as the "main chance" as we say, and small blame to him! He never at any rate looked towards literature: nor did the universities, wise in their generation, encourage him to do anything of the sort.

You may realise, Gentlemen, how tardily, even in later and more enlightened times, the study of Literature has crept its way into official Cambridge, if you will take down your *University Calendar* and study the list of professorships there set forth in order of foundation. It begins in 1502 with the Lady Margaret's Chair of Divinity, founded by the mother of Henry VII. Five Regius Professorships follow: of Divinity, Civil Law, Physic, Hebrew, Greek, all of 1540. So Greek comes in upon the flush of the Renaissance; and the *Calendar* bravely, yet not committing itself to a date, heads with Erasmus the noble roll which concludes (as may it long conclude) with Henry Jackson. But Greek comes in last of the five. Close on a hundred years elapse before the foundation of the next chair—it is of Arabic; and more than a hundred before we arrive at Mathematics. So Sir William Hamilton was not without historical excuse when he declared the study of Mathematics to be no part of the business of this University! Then follow Moral Philosophy (1683),

Music (1684), Chemistry (1702), Astronomy (1704), Anatomy (1707), Modern History and more Arabic, with Botany (1724), Geology (1727), closely followed by Mr. Hulse's Christian Advocate, more Astronomy (1749), more Divinity (1777), Experimental Philosophy (1783): then in the nineteenth century more Law, more Medicine, Mineralogy, Archaeology, Political Economy, Pure Mathematics, Comparative Anatomy, Sanskrit and yet again more Law, before we arrive in 1869 at a Chair of Latin. Faint yet pursuing, we have yet to pass chairs of Fine Art (belated), Experimental Physics, Applied Mechanics, Anglo-Saxon, Animal Morphology, Surgery, Physiology, Pathology, Ecclesiastical History, Chinese, more Divinity, Mental Philosophy, Ancient History, Agriculture, Biology, Agricultural Botany, more Biology, Astrophysics, and German, before arriving in 1910 at a chair of English Literature which by this time I have no breath to defend.

The enumeration has, I hope, been instructive. If it has also plunged you in gloom, to that atmosphere (as the clock warns me) for a fortnight I must leave you: with a promise, however, in another lecture to cheer you, if it may be, with some broken gleams of hope.

XI

English Literature in our Universities (II).

WE broke off, Gentlemen, upon the somewhat painful conclusion that our Universities were not founded for the study of literature, and tardily admitted it. The dates of our three literary chairs in Cambridge—I speak of our Western literature only, and omit Arabic, Sanskrit, and Chinese—clenched that conclusion for us. Greek in 1540, Latin not until 1869, English but three years ago—from the lesson of these intervals there is no getting away.

Now I do not propose to dwell on the Renaissance and how Greek came in: for a number of writers in our time have been busy with the Renaissance, and have—I was going to say "over-written the subject," but no—it is better to say that they have focussed the period so as to distort the general perspective at the cost of other periods which have earned less attention; the twelfth century, for example. At any rate their efforts, with the amount they claim of your reading, absolve me from doing more than remind you that the Renaissance brought in the study of Greek, and Greek necessarily brought in the study of literature: since no man can read what the Greeks wrote and not have his eyes unsealed to what I have called a norm of human expression; a guide to conduct, a standard to correct our efforts, whether in poetry, or in philosophy, or in art. For the rest, I need only quote to you Gibbon's magnificent saying, that the Greek language gave a soul to the objects of sense and a body to the abstractions of metaphysics. [May I add, in parenthesis, that, while no believer in compulsory Greek, holding, indeed, that you can hardly reconcile learning with compulsion, and still more hardly force them to be compatibles, I subscribe with all my heart to Bagehot's shrewd saying, "while a knowledge of Greek and Latin is not necessary to a writer of English, he should at least have a firm conviction that those two languages existed."]

But, assuming you to know something of the Renaissance, and how it brought Greek into Oxford and Cambridge, I find that in the course of the argument two things fall to be said, and both to be said with some emphasis.

In the first place, without officially acknowledging their native tongue or its literature, our two Universities had no sooner acquired Greek than their members became immensely interested in English. Take, for one witness out of many, Gabriel Harvey, Fellow of Pembroke Hall. His letters to Edmund Spenser have been preserved, as you know. Now Gabriel Harvey was a man whom few will praise, and very few could have loved. Few will quarrel with Dr. Courthope's description of him as "a person of considerable intellectual force, but intolerably arrogant and conceited, and with a taste vitiated by all the affectations of Italian humanism," or deny that "his tone in his published correspondence with Spenser is that of an intellectual bully."[1] None will refuse him the title of fool for attempting to mislead Spenser into writing hexameters. But all you can urge against Gabriel Harvey, on this count or that or the other, but accumulates proof that this donnish man was all the while giving thought—giving even ferocious thought—to the business of making an English Literature.

Let me adduce more pleasing evidence. On or about Christmas, in the year 1597, there was enacted here in Cambridge, in the hall of St. John's College, a play called *The Pilgrimage to Parnassus*,

[1] *Cambridge History of English Literature*, vol. iii, p. 241.

a skittish work, having for subject the "discontent of scholars"; the misery attending those who, unsupported by a private purse, would follow after poetry and culture. No one knows the author's name: but he had a wit which has kept something of its salt to this day, and in Christmas, 1597, it took Cambridge by storm. The public demanded a sequel, and *The Return from Parnassus* made its appearance on the following Christmas (again in St. John's College hall); to be followed by a *Second Part of the Return from Parnassus*, the author's overflow of wit, three years later. Of the popularity of the first and second plays—*The Pilgrimage* and *The Return, Part I*—we have good evidence in the prologue to *The Return, Part II*, where the author makes Momus say, before an audience which knew the truth:

> *The Pilgrimage to Parnassus* and *The Returne from Parnassus* have stood the honest Stagekeepers in many a crowne's expense for linckes and vizards: purchased many a Sophister a knocke with a clubbe: hindred the buttler's box, and emptied the Colledge barrells; and now, unlesse you have heard the former, you may returne home as wise as you came: for this last is the last part of *The Returne from Parnassus;* that is, the last time that the Author's wit will turne upon the toe in this vaine.

In other words, these plays had set everybody

in Cambridge agog, had been acted by link-light, had led to brawls—either between literary factions or through offensive personal allusions to which we have lost all clue—had swept into the box-office much money usually spent on Christmas gambling, and had set up an inappeasable thirst for College ale. The point for us is that (in 1597–1601) they abound in topical allusions to the London theatres: that Shakespeare is obviously just as much a concern to these young men of Cambridge as Mr. Shaw (say) is to our young men to-day, and an allusion to him is dropped in confidence that it will be aptly taken. For instance, one of the characters, Gullio, will have some love-verses recited to him "in two or three diverse veins, in Chaucer's, Gower's and Spenser's and Mr. Shakespeare's." Having listened to Chaucer, he cries, "Tush! Chaucer is a foole"; but coming to some lines of Mr. Shakespeare's *Venus and Adonis*, he cries, "Ey, marry, Sir! these have some life in them! Let this duncified world esteeme of Spenser and Chaucer, I'le worship sweet Mr. Shakespeare, and to honoure him I will lay his *Venus and Adonis* under my pillowe." For another allusion—"Few of the University pen plaies well," says the actor Kempe in Part II of the *Returne;* "they smell too much of that writer *Ovid* and that writer *Metamorphosis*, and talke too much of Proserpina and Jupiter. Why here's our fellow *Shakespeare* puts them all downe, ay and *Ben Jonson*, too." Here you have Cambridge assembling at Christmas-tide to laugh at well-understood hits upon the theatrical taste of London. Here you have, to make Cambridge laugh, three farcical quasi-Aristophanic plays all hinging on the tribulations of scholars who depart to pursue literature for a livelihood. For a piece of definite corroborative evidence you have a statute of Queens' College (quoted by Mr. Bass Mullinger) which directs that "any student refusing to take part in the acting of a comedy or tragedy in the College and absenting himself from the performance, contrary to the injunctions of the President, shall be expelled from the Society" —which seems drastic. And on top of all this, you have evidence enough and to spare of the part played in Elizabethan drama by the "University Wits." Why, Marlowe (of Corpus Christi) may be held to have invented its form—blank verse; Ben Jonson (of St. John's) to have carried it on past its meridian and through its decline, into the masque. Both Universities claim Lyly and Chapman. Marston, Peel, Massinger, hailed from Oxford. But Greene and Nashe were of Cambridge—of St. John's both, and Day of Caius.

They sought to London, and there (for tragic truth underlay that Christmas comedy of *The Pilgrimage to Parnassus*) many of them came to bitter ends: but before reaching their sordid personal ruin—and let the deaths of Marlowe and Greene be remembered—they built the Elizabethan drama, as some of them lived to add its last ornaments. We know what, meanwhile, Spenser had done. I think it scarcely needs further proof that Cambridge, towards the end of the sixteenth century, was fermenting with a desire to read, criticise, yes and *write*, English literature, albeit officially the University recognised no such thing.

There remains a second question—How happened it that Cambridge, after admitting Greek, took more than three hundred years to establish a Chair of Latin, and that a Chair of English is, so to speak, a mushroom (call it not toadstool!) of yesterday? Why simply enough. Latin continued to be the working language of Science. In Latin Bacon naturally composed his *Novum Organum* and indeed almost all his scientific and philosophical work, although a central figure of his age among English prose-writers. In Latin, in the eighteenth century, Newton wrote his *Principia:* and I suppose that of no two books written by Englishmen before the close of that century, or indeed before Darwin's *Origin of Species*, can it be less extravagantly said than of the *Novum Organum* and the *Principia* that they shook the world. Now, without forgetting our Classical Tripos (founded in 1822), as without forgetting the great names of Bentley and Porson, we may observe it as generally true, that whenever and wherever large numbers of scientific men use a particular language as their working instrument, they have a disposition to look askance on its refinements; to be jealous of its literary professors; to accuse these of treating as an end in itself what is properly a means. Like the Texas editor I quoted to you in a previous lecture, these scientific workers want to "get there" in a hurry, forgetting that (to use another Americanism) the sharper the chisel the more ice it is likely to cut. You may observe this disposition—this suspicion of "literature," this thinly veiled contempt—in many a scientific man to-day; though because his language has changed from Latin to English, it is English he now chooses to cheapen. Well, we cannot help it, perhaps. Perhaps he cannot help it. It is human nature. We must go on persuading him, not losing our tempers.

None the less we should not shut our eyes to the fact that while a language is the working instrument of scientific men there will always be a number of them to decry any study of it for its beauty, and even any study of it for the sake of accuracy—its beauty and its accuracy being indeed scarcely distinguishable.

I fear, Gentlemen, you may go on from this to the dreadful conclusion that the date 1869, when Cambridge at length came to possess a Chair of Latin, marks definitely the hour at which Latin closed its eyes and became a dead language; that you may proceed to a yet more dreadful application of this to the Chair of English founded in 1910: and that henceforward (to misquote what Mr. Max Beerbohm once wickedly said of Walter Pater) you will be apt to regard Professor Housman and me as two widowers engaged, while the undertaker waits, in composing the features of our belovèds.

But (to speak seriously) that is what I stand here to controvert: and I derive no small encouragement when—as has more than once happened—A, a scientific man, comes to me and complains that he for his part cannot understand B, another scientific man, "because the fellow can't express himself." And the need to study precision in writing has grown far more instant since men of science have abandoned the "universal language" and taken to writing in their own tongues. Let us, while not on the whole regretting the change, at least recognise some dangers, some possible disadvantages. I will confine myself to English, considered as a substitute for Latin. In Latin you have a language which may be thin in its vocabulary and inelastic for modern use; but a language which at all events compels a man to clear his thought and communicate it to other men precisely.

> Thoughts hardly to be packed
> Into the narrow act

—may be all impossible of compression into the Latin speech. In English, on the other hand, you have a language which by its very copiousness and elasticity tempts you to believe that you can do without packing, without compression, arrangement, order; that, with the Texas editor, all you need is to "get there"—though it be with all your intellectual belongings in a jumble, overflowing the portmanteau. Rather I preach to you that having proudly inherited English with its *copia fandi*, you should keep your estate in order by constantly applying to it that *jus et norma loquendi* of which, if you seek to the great models, you will likewise find yourselves inheritors.

"But," it is sometimes urged, "why not leave tnis new study of English to the younger universities now being set up all over the country?" "Ours is an age of specialising. Let these newcomers have something—what better than English?—to specialise upon."

I might respond by asking if the fame of Cambridge would stand where it stands to-day had she followed a like counsel concerning other studies and, resting upon Mathematics, given over this or that branch of Natural Science to be grasped by new hands. What of Electricity, for example? Or what of Physiology? Yes, and among the unnatural sciences, what of Political Economy? But I will use a more philosophical argument.

Some years ago I happened on a collection of Bulgarian proverbs of which my memory retains but two, yet each an abiding joy. In a lecture on English Literature in our Universities you will certainly not miss to apply the first, which runs, "Many an ass has entered Jerusalem."

The application of the second may elude you for a moment. It voices the impatience of an honest Bulgar who has been worried overmuch to subscribe to what, in this England of ours, we call Church Purposes; and it runs, "All these twopenny saints will be the ruin of the Church."

Now far be it from me to apply the term "twopenny saint" to any existing university. To avoid the accusation I hereby solemnly declare my deep conviction that every single university at this moment in England, Scotland, Wales, or Ireland has reasons—strong in all, in some overwhelmingly strong—for its existence. That is plainly said, I hope? Yet I do maintain that if we go on multiplying universities we shall not increase the joy; that the reign of two-penny saints lies not far off and will soon lie within measurable distance; and that it will be a pestilent reign. As we saw in our last lecture the word "university" —*universitas*—had, in its origin, nothing to do with universality: it meant no more than a society, organized (as it happened) to promote learning. But words, like institutions, often rise above their beginnings, and in time acquire a proud secondary connotation. For an instance let me give you the beautiful Wykehamist motto, *Manners Makyth Man*, wherein "manners" originally meant no more than "morals." So there has grown around our two great Universities of Oxford and Cambridge a connotation (secondary, if you will, but valuable above price) of universality; of standing like great beacons of light, to attract the young wings of all who would seek learning for their sustenance. Thousands have singed, thousands have burned themselves, no doubt: but what thousands of thousands have caught the sacred fire into their souls as they passed through and passed out, to carry it, to drop it, still as from wings, upon waste places of the world! Think of country vicarages, of Australian or Himalayan outposts, where men have nourished out lives of duty upon the fire of three transient, priceless years. Think of the generations of children to whom their fathers' lives, prosaic enough, could always be re-illumined if someone let fall the word "Oxford" or "Cambridge," so that they themselves came to surmise an aura about the name as of a land very far off; and then say if the ineffable spell of those two words do not lie somewhere in the conflux of generous youth with its rivalries and clash of minds, ere it disperses, generation after generation, to the duller business of life. Would you have your mother University, Gentlemen, undecorated by some true study of your mother-English?

I think not, having been there, and known such thoughts as you will carry away, and having been against expectation called back to report them.

And sometimes I remember days of old
When fellowship seem'd not so far to seek,
And all the world and I seem'd far less cold,
And at the rainbow's foot lay surely gold,
And hope was strong, and life itself not weak.

My purpose here (and I cannot too often recur to it) is to wean your minds from hankering after false Germanic standards and persuade you, or at least point out to you, in what direction that true study lies if you are men enough to take up your inheritance and believe in it as a glory to be improved.

Neither Oxford nor Cambridge nor any university on earth can study English Literature truthfully or worthily, or even at all profitably, unless by studying it in the category for which Heaven, or Nature (call the ultimate cause what you will), intended it; or, to put the assertion more concretely, in any other category than that for which the particular author—be his name Chaucer or Chesterton, Shakespeare or Shaw—designed it; as neither can Oxford nor Cambridge nor any university study English Literature, to understand it, unless by bracing itself to consider a living art. Origins, roots, all the gropings towards light—let these be granted as accessories; let those who search in them be granted all honour, all respect. It is only when they preach or teach these preliminaries, these accessories, to be more important than Literature itself—it is only when they, owing all their excuse in life to the established daylight, din upon us that the precedent darkness claims precedence in honour, that one is driven to utter upon them this dialogue, in monosyllables:

And God said, "Let there be light": and there was light.

"Oh, thank you, Sir," said the Bat and the Owl; "then we are off!"

I grant you, Gentlemen, that there must always inhere a difficulty in correlating for the purposes of a Tripos a study of Literature itself with a study of these accessories; the thing itself being *naturally* so much more difficult: being so difficult indeed that (to take literary criticism alone and leave for a moment the actual practice of writing out of the question) though some of the first intellects in the world—Aristotle, Longinus, Quintilian, Boileau, Dryden, Lessing, Goethe, Coleridge, Sainte-Beuve—have broken into parcels of that territory, the mass of it remains unexplored, and nobody as yet has found courage to reduce the reports of these great explorers to any system; so that a very eminent person indeed found it easy to write to me the other day, "The principles of Criticism? What are they? Who made them?" To this I could only answer that I did not know Who made them; but that Aristotle, Dryden, Lessing, had, as it was credibly reported, discovered five, or, it might be, six. And this difficulty of appraising literature absolutely inheres in your study of it from the beginning. No one can have set a General Paper on Literature and examined on it, setting it and marking the written answers, alongside of papers about language, inflexions, and the rest, without having borne in upon him that *here* the student finds his difficulty. While in a paper set about inflexions, etc., a pupil with a moderately retentive memory will easily obtain sixty or seventy per cent. of the total marks, in a paper on the book or play considered critically an examiner, even after setting his paper with a view to some certain inferiority of average, has to be lenient before he can award fifty, forty, or even thirty per cent. of the total.

You will find a somewhat illuminating passage —illuminating, that is, if you choose to interpret and apply it to our subject—in Lucian's *True History*, where the veracious traveller, who tells the tale, affirms that he visited Hades among other places, and had some conversation with Homer, among its many inhabitants.—

Before many days had passed, I accosted the poet Homer, when we were both disengaged, and asked him, among other things, where he came from; it was still a burning question with us, I explained. He said he was aware that some derived him from Chios, others from Smyrna, and others again from Colophon; but in fact he was a Babylonian, generally known not as Homer but as Tigranes; but when later in life he was given as a *homer* or hostage to the Greeks, that name clung to him. Another of my questions was about the so-called spurious books; had he written them or not? He said that they were all genuine: so I now knew what to think of the critics Zenodotus and Aristarchus and all their lucubrations. Having got a categorical answer on that point, I tried him next on his reason for starting the *Iliad* with the wrath of Achilles. He said he had no exquisite reason; it just came into his head that way.

Even so diverse are the questions that may be asked concerning any great work of art. But to discover its full intent is always the most difficult task of all. That task, however, and nothing less difficult, will always be the one worthiest of a great university.

On that, and on that alone, Gentlemen, do I base all claims for our School of English Literature. And yet in conclusion I will ask you, reminding yourselves how fortunate is your lot in Cambridge, to think of fellow-Englishmen far less fortunate.

Years ago I took some pains to examine the examination papers set by a renowned Examining

Body and I found *this*—"I humbly solicit" (to use a phrase of Lucian's) "my hearers' incredulity"—that in a paper set upon three Acts of *Hamlet*—three Acts of *Hamlet!*—the first question started with "G.tt. p..cha" "Al..g.tor" and invited the candidate to fill in the missing letters correctly. Now I was morally certain that the words "gutta-percha" and "alligator" did not occur in the first three Acts of *Hamlet;* but having carefully re-read them I invited this examining body to explain itself. The answer I got was that, to understand Shakespeare, a student must first understand the English Language! Some of you on leaving Cambridge will go out—a company of Christian folk dispersed throughout the world—to tell English children of English Literature. Such are the pedagogic fetters you will have to knock off their young minds before they can stand and walk.

Gentlemen, on a day early in this term I sought the mound which is the old Castle of Cambridge. Access to it, as perhaps you know, lies through the precincts of the County Prison. An iron railing encloses the mound, having a small gate, for the key of which a notice-board advised me to ring the prison bell. I rang. A very courteous gaoler answered the bell and opened the gate, which stands just against his wicket. I thanked him, but could not forbear asking, "Why do they keep this gate closed?" "I don't know, sir," he answered, "but I suppose if they didn't the children might get in and play."

So with his answer I went up the hill and from the top saw Cambridge spread at my feet; Magdalene below me, and the bridge which—poor product as it is of the municipal taste—has given its name to so many bridges all over the world; the river on its long ambit to Chesterton; the tower of St. John's, and beyond it the unpretentious but more beautiful tower of Jesus College. To my right the magnificent chine of King's College Chapel made its own horizon above the yellowing elms. I looked down on the streets—the narrow streets—the very streets which, a fortnight ago, I tried to people for you with that mediaeval throng which has passed as we shall pass. Still in my ear the gaoler's answer repeated itself—"*I suppose, if they didn't keep it locked, the children might get in and play*": and a broken echo seemed to take it up, in words that for a while had no more coherence than the scattered jangle of bells in the town below. But as I turned to leave, they chimed into an articulate sentence and the voice was the voice of Francis Bacon—*Regnum Scientiae ut reg-*

num Coeli non nisi sub persona infantis intratur.—Into the Kingdom of Knowledge, as into the Kingdom of Heaven, whoso would enter must become as a little child.

XII

On Style

SHOULD Providence, Gentlemen, destine any one of you to write books for his living, he will find experimentally true what I here promise him, that few pleasures sooner cloy than reading what the reviewers say. This promise I hand on with the better confidence since it was endorsed for me once in conversation by that eminently good man the late Henry Sidgwick; who added, however, "Perhaps I ought to make a single exception. There was a critic who called one of my books 'epoch-making.' Being anonymous, he would have been hard to find and thank, perhaps; but I ought to have made the effort."

May I follow up this experience of his with one of my own, as a preface or brief apology for this lecture? Short-lived as is the author's joy in his critics, far-spent as may be his hope of fame, mournful his consent with Sir Thomas Browne that "there is nothing immortal but immortality," he cannot hide from certain sanguine men of business, who in England call themselves "Press-Cutting Agencies," in America "Press-Clipping Bureaus," and, as each successive child of his invention comes to birth, unbecomingly presume in him an almost virginal trepidation. "Your book," they write falsely, "is exciting much comment. May we collect and send you notices of it appearing in the World's Press? We submit a specimen cutting with our terms; and are, dear Sir," etc.

Now, although steadily unresponsive to this wile, I am sometimes guilty of taking the enclosed specimen review and thrusting it for preservation among the scarcely less deciduous leaves of the book it was written to appraise. So it happened that having this vacation, to dust—not to read—a line of obsolete or obsolescent works on a shelf, I happened on a review signed by no smaller a man than Mr. Gilbert Chesterton and informing the world that the author of my obsolete book was full of good stories as a kindly uncle, but had a careless or impatient way of stopping short and leaving his readers to guess what they most wanted to know: that, reaching the last chapter, or what he chose to make the last chapter, instead of winding up and telling "how everybody lived ever after," he (so to speak) slid you off his avuncular knee with a blessing and the remark that nine o'clock was striking and all good children should be in their beds.

That criticism has haunted me during the vacation. Looking back on a course of lectures which I deemed to be accomplished; correcting them in print; revising them with all the nervousness of a beginner; I have seemed to hear you complain—"He has exhorted us to write accurately, appropriately; to eschew Jargon; to be bold and essay Verse. He has insisted that Literature is a living art, to be practised. But just what we most needed he has not told. At the final doorway to the secret he turned his back and left us. Accuracy, propriety, perspicuity—these we may achieve. But where has he helped us to write with beauty, with charm, with distinction? Where has he given us rules for what is called *Style* in short?—having attained which an author may count himself set up in business."

Thus, Gentlemen, with my mind's ear I heard you reproaching me. I beg you to accept what follows for my apology.

To begin with, let me plead that you have been told of one or two things which Style is *not;* which have little or nothing to do with Style, though sometimes vulgarly mistaken for it. Style, for example, is not—can never be—extraneous Ornament. You remember, may be, the Persian lover whom I quoted to you out of Newman: how to convey his passion he sought a professional letter-writer and purchased a vocabulary charged with ornament, wherewith to attract the fair one as with a basket of jewels. Well, in this extraneous, professional, purchased ornamentation, you have something which Style *is not:* and if you here require a practical rule of me, I will present you with this: "Whenever you feel an impulse to perpetrate a piece of exceptionally fine writing, obey it—whole-heartedly—and delete it before sending your manuscript to press. *Murder your darlings.*"

But let me plead further that you have not been left altogether without clue to the secret of what Style *is.* That you must master the secret for yourselves lay implicit in our bargain, and you were never promised that a writer's training would be easy. Yet a clue was certainly put in your hands when, having insisted that Literature is a living art, I added that therefore it must be personal and of its essence personal.

This goes very deep: it conditions all our criticism of art. Yet it conceals no mystery. You may see its meaning most easily and clearly, perhaps, by contrasting Science and Art at their two extremes—say Pure Mathematics with Acting. Science as a rule deals with things, Art with man's thought and emotion about things. In Pure Mathematics things are rarefied into ideas, numbers, concepts, but still farther and farther away from the individual man. Two and two make four, and fourpence is not ninepence (or at any rate four is not nine) whether Alcibiades or Cleon keep the tally. In Acting on the other hand almost everything depends on personal interpretation—on the gesture, the walk, the gaze, the tone of a Siddons, the *rusé* smile of a Coquelin, the exquisite, vibrant intonation of a Bernhardt. "English Art?" exclaimed Whistler, "there is no such thing! Art is art and mathematics is mathematics." Whistler erred. Precisely because Art is Art, and Mathematics is Mathematics and a Science, Art being Art can be English or French; and, more than this, must be the personal expression of an Englishman or a Frenchman, as a "Constable" differs from a "Corot" and a "Whistler" from both. Surely I need not labour this. But what is true of the extremes of Art and Science is true also, though sometimes less recognisably true, of the mean: and where they meet and seem to conflict (as in History) the impact is that of the personal or individual mind upon universal truth, and the question becomes whether what happened in the Sicilian Expedition, or at the trial of Charles I, can be set forth naked as an algebraical sum, serene in its certainty, indifferent to opinion, uncoloured in the telling as in the hearing by sympathy or dislike, by passion or by character. I doubt, while we should strive in history as in all things to be fair, if history can be written in that colourless way, to interest men in human doings. I am sure that nothing which lies further towards imaginative, creative Art can be written in that way.

It follows then that Literature, being by its nature personal, must be by its nature almost infinitely various. "Two persons cannot be the authors of the sounds which strike our ear; and as they cannot be speaking one and the same speech, neither can they be writing one and the same lecture or discourse." *Quot homines tot sententiae.* You may translate that, if you will, "Every man of us constructs his sentences differently"; and if there be indeed any quarrel between Literature and Science (as I never can see why there should be), I for one will readily grant Science all her cold superiority, her ease in Sion with universal facts, so it be mine to serve among the multifarious race who have to adjust, as best they may, Science's cold conclusions (and much else) to the brotherly give-and-take of human life.

Quicquid agunt homines, votum, timor, ira, voluptas . . . Is it possible, Gentlemen, that you can have read one, two, three, or more of the acknowledged masterpieces of literature without having it borne in on you that they are great because they are alive, and traffic not with cold celestial certainties, but with men's hopes, aspirations, doubts, loves, hates, breakings of the heart; the glory and vanity of human endeavour, the transience of beauty, the capricious uncertain lease on which you and I hold life, the dark coast to which we inevitably steer; all that amuses or vexes, all that gladdens, saddens, maddens us men and women on this brief and mutable traject which yet must be home for a while, the anchorage of our hearts? For an instance:—

Here lies a most beautiful lady,
  Light of step and heart was she:
I think she was the most beautiful lady
  That ever was in the West Country.

But beauty vanishes, beauty passes,
  However rare, rare it be;
And when I crumble who shall remember
  That lady of the West Country?[1]

[1] Walter de la Mare.

Or take a critic—a literary critic—such as Samuel Johnson, of whom we are used to think as of a man artificial in phrase and pedantic in judgment. He lives, and why? Because, if you test his criticism, he never saw literature but as a part of life, nor would allow in literature what was false to life, as he saw it. He could be wrong-headed, perverse; could damn Milton because he hated Milton's politics; on any question of passion or prejudice could make injustice his daily food. But he could not, even in a friend's epitaph, let pass a phrase (however well turned) which struck him as empty of life or false to it. All Boswell testifies to this: and this is why Samuel Johnson survives.

Now let me carry this contention—that all Literature is personal and therefore various—into a field much exploited by the pedant, and fenced about with many notice-boards and public warnings. "*Neologisms not allowed here.*" "*All persons using slang, or trespassing in pursuit of originality. . . .*"

Well, I answer these notice-boards by saying that, literature being personal, and men various—and even the *Oxford English Dictionary* being no Canonical book—man's use or defiance of the dictionary depends for its justification on nothing but his success: adding that, since it takes all kinds to make a world, or a literature, his success will probably depend on the occasion. A few months ago I found myself seated at a bump-supper next to a cheerful youth who, towards the close, suggested thoughtfully, as I arose to make a speech, that, the bonfire (which of course he called the "bonner") being due at nine-thirty o'clock, there was little more than bare time left for "langers and godders." It cost me, who think slowly, some seconds to interpret that by "langers" he meant "Auld Lang Syne" and by "godders" "God Save the King." I thought at the time, and still think, and will maintain against any schoolmaster, that the neologisms of my young neighbour, though not to be recommended for essays or sermons, did admirably suit the time, place, and occasion.

Seeing that in human discourse, infinitely varied as it is, so much must ever depend on *who* speaks, and to *whom*, in what mood and upon what occasion; and seeing that Literature must needs take account of all manner of writers, audiences, moods, occasions; I hold it a sin against the light to put up a warning against any word that comes to us in the fair way of use and wont (as "wire," for instance, for a telegram), even as surely as we should warn off hybrids or deliberately pedantic impostors, such as "antibody" and "picture-drome"; and that, generally, it is better to err on the side of liberty than on the side of the censor: since by the manumitting of new words we infuse new blood into a tongue of which (or we have learnt nothing from Shakespeare's audacity) our first pride should be that it is flexible, alive, capable of responding to new demands of man's untiring quest after knowledge and experience. Not because it was an ugly thing did I denounce Jargon to you, the other day: but because it was a dead thing, leading nowhither, meaning naught. There is *wickedness* in human speech, sometimes. You will detect it all the better for having ruled out what is *naughty*.

Let us err, then, if we err, on the side of liberty. I came, the other day, upon this passage in Mr. Frank Harris's study of "The Man Shakespeare":—

In the last hundred years the language of Molière has grown fourfold; the slang of the studios and the gutter and the laboratory, of the engineering school and the dissecting table, has been ransacked for special terms to enrich and strengthen the language in order that it may deal easily with the new thoughts. French is now a superb instrument, while English is positively poorer than it was in the time of Shakespeare, thanks to the prudery of our illiterate middle class.[1]

Well, let us not lose our heads over this, any more than over other prophecies of our national decadence. The *Oxford English Dictionary* has not yet unfolded the last of its coils, which yet are ample enough to enfold us in seven words for every three an active man can grapple with. Yet the warning has point, and a particular point, for those who aspire to write poetry: as Francis Thompson has noted in his Essay on Shelley:—

> Theoretically, of course, one ought always to try for the best word. But practically, the habit of excessive care in word-selection frequently results in loss of spontaneity; and, still worse, the habit of always taking the best word too easily becomes the habit of always taking the most ornate word, the word most removed from ordinary speech. In conquence of this, poetic diction has become latterly a kaleidoscope, and one's chief curiosity is as to the precise combinations into which the pieces will be shifted. There is, in fact, a certain band of words, the Praetorian cohorts of Poetry, whose prescriptive aid is invoked by every aspirant to the poetic purple. . . . Against these it is time some banner should be raised.

[1] "An oration," says Quintilian, "may find room for almost any word saving a few indecent ones (*quae sunt parum verecunda*)." He adds that writers of the Old Comedy were often commended even for these: "but it is enough for us to mind our present business—*sed nobis nostrum opus intueri sat est.*"

. . It is at any rate curious to note that the literary revolution against the despotic diction of Pope seems issuing, like political revolutions, in a despotism of his own making;

and he adds a note that this is the more surprising to him because so many Victorian poets were prose-writers as well.

Now, according to our theory, the practice of prose should maintain fresh and comprehensive a poet's diction, should save him from falling into the hands of an exclusive coterie of poetic words. It should react upon his metrical vocabulary to its beneficial expansion, by taking him outside his aristocratic circle of language, and keeping him in touch with the great commonalty, the proletariat of speech. For it is with words as with men: constant intermarriage within the limits of a patrician clan begets effete refinement; and to reinvigorate the stock, its veins must be replenished from hardy plebeian blood.

In diction, then, let us acquire all the store we can, rejecting no coin for its minting but only if its metal be base. So shall we bring out of our treasuries new things and old.

Diction, however, is but a part of Style, and perhaps not the most important part. So I revert to the larger question, "What is Style? What its τὸ τί ἦν εἶναι, its essence, the law of its being?"

Now, as I sat down to write this lecture, memory evoked a scene and with the scene a chance word of boyish slang, both of which may seem to you irrelevant until, or unless, I can make you feel how they hold for me the heart of the matter.

I once happened to be standing in a corner of a ball-room when there entered the most beautiful girl these eyes have ever seen or now—since they grow dull—ever will see. It was, I believe, her first ball, and by some freak or in some premonition she wore black: and not pearls—which, I am told, maidens are wont to wear on these occasions—but one crescent of diamonds in her black hair. *Et vera incessu patuit dea.* Here, I say, was absolute beauty. It startled.

> I think she was the most beautiful lady
> That ever was in the West Country.
> But beauty vanishes, beauty passes. . . .

She died a year or two later. She may have been too beautiful to live long. I have a thought that she may also have been too good.

For I saw her with the crowd about her: I saw led up and presented among others the man who was to be, for a few months, her husband: and then, as the men bowed, pencilling on their programmes, over their shoulders I saw her eyes travel to an awkward young naval cadet (Do you remember Crossjay in Meredith's *The Egoist?* It was just such a boy) who sat abashed and glowering sulkily beside me on the far bench. Promptly with a laugh, she advanced, claimed him, and swept him off into the first waltz.

When it was over he came back, a trifle flushed, and I felicitated him; my remark (which I forget) being no doubt "just the sort of banality, you know, one does come out with"—as maybe that the British Navy kept its old knack of cutting out. But he looked at me almost in tears and blurted, "It isn't her beauty, sir. You saw? It's—it's—my God, it's the *style!*"

Now you may think that a somewhat cheap, or at any rate inadequate, cry of the heart in my young seaman; as you may think it inadequate in me, and moreover a trifle capricious, to assure you (as I do) that the first and last secret of a good Style consists in thinking with the heart as well as with the head.

But let us philosophise a little. You have been told, I daresay often enough, that the business of writing demands *two*—the author and the reader. Add to this what is equally obvious, that the obligation of courtesy rests first with the author, who invites the séance, and commonly charges for it. What follows, but that in speaking or writing we have an obligation to put ourselves into the hearer's or reader's place? It is *his* comfort, *his* convenience, we have to consult. To *express* ourselves is a very small part of the business: very small and almost unimportant as compared with *impressing* ourselves: the aim of the whole process being to persuade.

All reading demands an effort. The energy, the good-will which a reader brings to the book is, and must be, partly expended in the labour of reading, marking, learning, inwardly digesting what the author means. The more difficulties, then, we authors obtrude on him by obscure or careless writing, the more we blunt the edge of his attention: so that if only in our own interest—though I had rather keep it on the ground of courtesy—we should study to anticipate his comfort.

But let me go a little deeper. You all know that a great part of Lessing's argument in his *Laoköon*, on the essentials of Literature as opposed to Pictorial Art or Sculpture, depends on this—that in Pictorial Art or in Sculpture the eye sees, the mind apprehends, the whole in a moment of time, with the correspondent disadvantage that this moment of time is fixed and stationary; whereas in writing, whether in prose or in verse, we can only produce our effect by a series of successive small impressions, dripping our meaning (so to speak) into the reader's mind—with the correspondent advantage, in point of vivacity, that our picture keeps moving all the while. Now obviously this throws a greater strain on his patience whom we address. Man at the best is a narrow-mouthed bottle. Through the conduit of speech he can utter—as you, my hearers, can receive—only one word at a time. In writing (as my old friend Professor Minto used to say) you are as a commander filing out his battalion through a narrow gate that allows only one man at a time to pass; and your reader, as he receives the troops, has to reform and reconstruct them. No matter how large or how involved the subject, it can be communicated only in that way. You see, then, what an obligation we owe to him of order and arrangement; and why, apart from felicities and curiosities of diction, the old rhetoricians laid such stress upon order and arrangement as duties we owe to those who honour us with their attention. "*La clarté,*" says a French writer, "*est la politesse.*" Χάρισι καὶ σαφηνείᾳ θῦε, recommends Lucian. Pay your sacrifice to the Graces, and to σαφήνεια—Clarity—first among the Graces.

What am I urging? "That Style in writing is much the same thing as good manners in other human intercourse?" Well, and why not? At all events we have reached a point where Buffon's often-quoted saying that "Style is the man himself" touches and coincides with William of Wykeham's old motto that "Manners makyth Man"; and before you condemn my doctrine as inadequate listen to this from Coventry Patmore, still bearing in mind that a writer's main object is to *impress* his thought or vision upon his hearer.

"There is nothing comparable *for moral force* to the charm of truly noble manners. . . ."

I grant you, to be sure, that the claim to possess a Style must be conceded to many writers—Carlyle is one—who take no care to put listeners at their ease, but rely rather on native force of genius to shock and astound. Nor will I grudge them your admiration. But I do say that, as more and more you grow to value truth and the modest grace of truth, it is less and less to such writers that you will turn: and I say even more confidently that the qualities of Style we allow them are not the qualities we should seek as a norm, for they one and all offend against Art's true maxim of avoiding excess.

And this brings me to the two great *paradoxes* of Style. For the first (1),—although Style is so curiously personal and individual, and although men are so variously built that no two in the world carry away the same impressions from a show, there is always a norm somewhere; in literature and art, as in morality. Yes, even in man's most terrific, most potent inventions—when, for example, in *Hamlet* or *Lear* Shakespeare seems to be breaking up the solid earth under our feet—there is always some point and standard of sanity—a Kent or an Horatio—to which all enormities and passionate errors may be referred; to which the agitated mind of the spectator settles back as upon its centre of gravity, its pivot of repose.

(2) The second paradox, though it is equally true, you may find a little subtler. Yet it but applies to Art the simple truth of the Gospel, that he who would save his soul must first lose it. Though personality pervades Style and cannot be escaped, the first sin against Style as against good Manners is to obtrude or exploit personality. The very greatest work in Literature—the *Iliad*, the *Odyssey*, the *Purgatorio*, *The Tempest*, *Paradise Lost*, the *Republic*, *Don Quixote*—is all

> Seraphically free
> From taint of personality.

And Flaubert, that gladiator among artists, held that, at its highest, literary art could be carried into pure science. "I believe," said he, "that great art is scientific and impersonal. You should by an intellectual effort transport yourself into characters, not draw *them* into *yourself*. That at least is the method." On the other hand, says Goethe, "We should endeavour to use words that correspond as closely as possible with what *we* feel, see, think, imagine, experience, and reason. It is an endeavour we cannot evade and must daily renew." I call Flaubert's the better counsel, even though I have spent a part of this lecture in attempting to prove it impossible. It at least is noble, encouraging us to what is difficult. The shrewder Goethe encourages us to exploit ourselves to the top of our bent. I think Flaubert would have hit the mark if for "impersonal" he had substituted "disinterested."

For—believe me, Gentlemen—so far as Handel stands above Chopin, as Velasquez above Greuze, even so far stand the great masculine objective writers above all who appeal to you by parade of personality or private sentiment.

Mention of these great masculine "objective" writers brings me to my last word: which is, "Steep yourselves in *them:* habitually bring all to the test of *them:* for while you cannot escape the fate of all style, which is to be personal, the more of catholic manhood you inherit from those great loins the more you will assuredly beget."

This then is Style. As technically manifested in Literature it is the power to touch with ease grace, precision, any note in the gamut of human thought or emotion.

But essentially it resembles good manners. It comes of endeavouring to understand others, of thinking for them rather than for yourself—of thinking, that is, with the heart as well as the head. It gives rather than receives; it is nobly careless of thanks or applause, not being fed by these but rather sustained and continually refreshed by an inward loyalty to the best. Yet, like "character" it has its altar within; to that retires for counsel, from that fetches its illumination, to ray outwards. Cultivate, Gentlemen, that habit of withdrawing to be advised by the best. So, says Fénelon, "you will find yourself infinitely quieter, your words will be fewer and more effectual; and while you make less ado, what you do will be more profitable."

INDEX

Abelard, 245, 247, 255
Abercrombie, Lascelles, 21
Addison, Joseph, 151, 208
Alcuin, 239, 240, 246
Alfred, King, 225
Aristophanes, 231, 232
Aristotle, 154, 244, 272
Arnold, Matthew, 43, 92, 156, 224, 242
Arte of Rhetorique, Wilson's, 144
Ascham, Roger, 147, 226
Augustine, 238

Bacon, Lord, 7, 8, 12, 264, 276
Bagehot, Walter, 259
Ballata, 55
Barbour, John, 137
Barrie, Sir James Matthew, 21, 162
Bede, 245
Beerbohm, Max, 266
Belisarius, 212
Bentham, Jeremy, 117
Beowulf, 193–200
Béranger, Pierre-Jean de, 55
Berners, Lord, 131–134, 146
Bible, The: Authorized Version, 65, 117, 118, 148 *et seq.*, 170, 171, 174, 229; *Revised Version*, 159–160
Blair, Wilfred, 96
Blake, William, 15
Boccaccio, 222
Boëthius, 244
Bologna, University of, 241, 247
Borneil, Giraud de, 218
Boswell, James, 285
Bridges, Robert, 23
Brooke, the Rev. Stopford A., 193
Brougham, Lord, 56, 123
Browne, Sir Thomas, 12, 62, 151, 204, 278
Browning, Robert, 46, 224
Buffon, 294
Bunyan, John, 151
Burke, Edmund, 33, 56, 57–64, 122, 123
Burns, Robert, 55
Butler, Arthur John, 24

Cædmon, 198
Cambridge, 241 *et seq.*
Campion, Thomas, 223, 227
Carducci, Giosué, 187–188
Carlyle, Thomas, 22, 125, 294
Cellini, Benvenuto, 48
Cervantes, 9, 30
Chadwick, Professor H. M., 197
Chair of English Literature, University Ordinance, 8, 9
Chambers, E. K., 239
Champeaux, William of, 247
Chaucer, Geoffrey, 12, 134–136, 198, 221, 222, 262
Chesterton, Gilbert K., 279
Chichester, Richard of, 254
Cicero, 34, 60
Clare, John, 47
Coleridge, Samuel Taylor, 48, 77, 78, 79
Conington, John, 208
Courthope, W. J., 16, 192, 223, 239
Coverdale, Miles, 151

Cowley, Abraham, 224
Cowper, William, 224
Crewe, Lord Chief Justice, 8
Cynewulf, 198

Daniel, Samuel, 223, 227
Dante, 94, 222
Darwin, Charles, 265
Defoe, Daniel, 75, 91
Dekker, Thomas, 79
De la Mare, Walter, 284
De Quincey, Thomas, 66
Desiderius, Archbishop, 240
Dionysius of Halicarnassus, 34
Donne, John, 124, 129, 223
Dryden, John, 208, 224, 272
Duchess of Malfy, Webster's, 121
Dunbar, 12

"Eliot, George," 13
Emerson, Ralph Waldo, 13

Falconer, William, 95
Falkner, J. Meade, 203–204
Fénelon, 297
FitzGerald, Edward, 117
Flaubert, Gustave, 295, 296
Fletcher, John, 16
Fowler, H. W. and F. G., 109, 166, 167
Freeman, Professor E. A., 192, 194, 211–216, 225
Froissart, Berners', 131, 132
Froude, James Anthony, 95
Fuller, Thomas, 248

Gibbon, Edward, 151, 259
Gildas, 211
Goethe, 125, 296
Gray, Thomas, 13, 19, 163, 191–192, 197
Green, J. R., 192
Green, T. H., 10
Gregory the Great, Pope, 239, 240
Grierson, Professor H. J. C., 223

Hamilton, Sir William, 256
Hardy, Thomas, 21
Harris, Frank, 287
Harvey, Gabriel, 223, 260
Heine, Heinrich, 55
Herbert, George, 160
Hero and Leander, Marlowe's, 118, 119
Herodotus, 53, 77
Homer, 30, 77, 84, 92–94, 96–98, 195, 229, 273–274
Horace, 207–208
Housman, Professor A. E., 266

Ibsen, 117
Irnerius, 247
Isaiah, 157–160

Jackson, Dr. Henry, 256
Johnson, Samuel, 13, 14, 45, 83, 84, 148, 208, 285
Jonson, Ben, 155, 177, 223, 263
Jowett, Benjamin, 35
Jusserand, J. J., 220
Juvenal, 208–209

Keats, John, 19, 47, 224
Kempis, Thomas à, 18
Ker, Professor W. P., 194, 239
Kipling, Rudyard, 74

Lamb, Charles, 49
Lessing, 98, 272, 292
Lindsay, the Rev. T. M., D.D., 144
Lloyd George, the Right Hon. David, 165–166
Lucian, 7, 194, 231, 273, 293
Lucretius, 233

Malory, Sir Thomas, 130–134, 146
Marlowe, Christopher, 118–121, 223, 263
Marvell, Andrew, 224
Mason, William, 191
Masson, David, 15
McKenna, the Right Hon. Reginald, 164–165
Meredith, George, 291

Milton, John, 1, 12, 19, 52, 68–75, 89–92, 151, 184, 223, 235, 285
Minto, Professor William, 293
Moore, Thomas, 55
Morris, William, 227
Mullinger, J. Bass, 246, 263
Murray, Professor Gilbert, 232

Nashe, Thomas, 146
Newman, Cardinal, 6, 36, 37–39, 140, 141, 161, 173, 178, 281
Newton, Sir Isaac, 264
Noyes, Alfred, 95
Nut-Brown Maid, The, 136

Oates, Captain, 50
Origen, 235, 243
Oxford, 241 *et seq.*

Paris, University of, 241, 247
Pater, Walter, 93, 266
Patmore, Coventry, 294
Payne, E. J., 122, 124
Pervigilium Veneris, 183, 233
Pheidias, 17
Philosophy and Poetry, 1
Piers Plowman, 198, 220
Pilgrimage to Parnassus, The, 260–264
Plato, 1–5, 183, 246
Pliny, 184–186
Podsnap (*see* Freeman)
Poggio, 246
Pope, Alexander, 190, 191, 197
Powell, F. York, 193
Provençal Song, 218–221
Pythagoras, 250

Quintilian, 35, 168, 288

Raleigh, Professor Sir Walter, 11
Rashdall, Hastings, 250–252
Remigius, 247
Renan, 1
Reynolds, Sir Joshua, 28–29

Sainte-Beuve, Charles Augustus, 24
Saintsbury, Prof. George, 66–68, 225
Salamanca, University of, 241
Scott, The Antarctic Expedition, 50, 51
Severus, Sulpicius, 239
Shakespeare, William, 18, 19, 30, 60, 61, 62–63, 118–122, 138, 155, 156, 223, 229, 237, 262, 263, 275, 295
Shaw, George Bernard, 87
Shelley, 48
Shirley, James, 129
Sidgwick, Henry, 278
Sidney, Sir Philip, 50
Skeat, Walter W., 15
Sonata, 55
South, Robert, 124
Spenser, Edmund, 223, 248, 260, 262
Stevenson, Robert Louis, 160
Stubbs, Bishop W., 54
"Student's Handbook, The," 87–88
Swift, Jonathan, 75
Swinburne, Algernon, 236

Taylor, Jeremy, 83–84
Tennyson, Lord, 90, 91, 224
Tertullian, 235, 238, 243
Thackeray, William Makepeace, 152
Thompson, Francis, 288
Thomson, James, 47
Toulouse, University of, 250
Tyndale, William, 148, 153, 154

Vacarius, 247
Ventadour, Bernard de, 218, 219
Venus and Adonis, 118–120
Verrall, Dr. A. W., 8
Vigfússon, Gudbrand, 193
Virgil, 30, 97, 233, 240
Voltaire, 231

Waller, Edmund, 1

Walpole, Horatio, 209
Walton, Isaak, 84–86, 151, 242
Warton, Thomas, 191, 192
Watson, E. J., 188
Watson, William, 19, 20
Webster, John, 121
Wendell, Barrett, 118
Whistler, James McNeill, 282
Whitman, Walt, 64, 65, 68
Widsith, 72
Wolfe, General, 163
Wood, Anthony, 222
Wordsworth, William, 13, 14, 67, 81, 82, 154, 177, 224, 245, 253
Wright, Aldis, 15
Wyat, Sir Thomas, 140–144, 222
Wyclif, John, 151, 154

Yeats, William Butler, 171
Young, Arthur, 205